# THE HEALING ECHO

# THE
# HEALING ECHO

*by*

EUGENE HEIMLER

A CONDOR BOOK
SOUVENIR PRESS (E & A) LTD

ISBN 0 285 65008 4

Typeset by Inforum Ltd, Portsmouth
Printed in Great Britain by
Photobooks (Bristol) Ltd.

To the memory of Lily

# *Acknowledgements*

I want to express my thanks to Ted and Sharon Cardwell for having offered their old cottage at Emma Lake, Saskatchewan, Canada, where I started this book between snowstorms and mosquitoes.

My gratitude goes to Brigitte for her patience and encouragement while I was writing this book. She spent many hours conducting and transcribing interviews from tapes and helped me to shape the destiny of this writing with her advice and enthusiasm.

# Contents

The Age of Unemployment is on us. Work, as we have known it since the Industrial Revolution, is over, yet there does not appear to be a full recognition that we shall never return to the 'Bad Old Days'.

The new unemployed knows that the present crisis of change may herald new opportunities. The old unemployed is bewildered and confused.

It will take time before *the gift of unemployment* will be received; but when it is, we shall enter a totally different dimension of living. The creative existence of Man is now a real possibility, provided we can hear our healing echo.

E.H.
London, June 1985

# *Introduction*

I spent most of my professional life working with work and unemployment. I came across many men and women who loved their work, and many more who hated it, and some who either periodically or continuously had no work at all. Those who were deeply engaged in what they were doing and gained satisfaction from it were flowing with life, and those to whom their work was humdrum, difficult, boring or non-existent could not, and did not, experience life to the full. As I worked for over three decades in the field of emotional and mental health, it was not difficult to see how health and illness were often the result of purpose or the lack of it. Ageing, too, was not just a deteriorative or degenerative process of passing years, but depended upon involvement or non-involvement in living and remaining active or otherwise. Even sexual functioning was affected by *meaning* and *purpose*.

That work or purposeful activity could have such an extra-ordinary effect on people was a real eye opener to me. In time this line of professional activity became *my* purpose and meaning, and I learned how to assist others to find these in *their* lives.

My interest in unemployment, redundancy and stagnation goes back a long time. After the Nazis gained increasing influence in my native Hungary in the early 1940s, my father was not allowed to practise law, nor could he take part in political activities as an elected member of the County Council. In modern terms he became redundant. *My father was the first redundant person I ever came across in my life.* Within a year he acted, behaved and thought as if he were at least twenty years older. He also lost interest in practically everything, became very depressed, and sat all day by the window, oblivious of what was going on around him.

I believe that my concern with unemployment started when I impotently had to witness the totally useless existence thus imposed on my father by the National Socialists. Later, after the war, when I made my home in England, my interest in the unemployed re-awoke when I saw in my professional work so many men who, as a result of their wartime experiences, had received injuries (visible and invisible), and could not find work without considerable assistance. Like my father, they seemed to have lost interest in life and were often anxious and depressed. By helping them to find new meaning in their lives, I could at last do something; I could heal at least *their* apathy, even if I could not help my father any more. Today, having reached the age my father was then, I am still involved in trying to find new roads for the unemployed, the redundant, and those who feel that they are 'stuck' in a bad job.

The philosophy of my work, which has emerged slowly during the last decades, can be expressed in the following: *Our motivation does not necessarily grow from good or positive experiences; on the contrary, very often pain is the spur for and towards our meaningful activities in life. The question is not why the pain, but what is to be done with it.* My work is concerned with this 'what', and, after that, with how to do it. In this book I hope to answer both questions.

When I came to England in 1947, I myself went through a long period of unemployment, partly because it was difficult to obtain a work permit from the Home Office, and partly because I did not speak English. My emotional experiences as a young unemployed man in the late 1940s were no different from those of any unemployed men and women today. I experienced a sense of being lost; I felt of little value – in many ways completely worthless. I kept saying to myself that I should not have these feelings, that things would eventually improve, but deep down I had doubt and considerable depression. With a dictionary in my hand I sat in libraries reading job advertisements, yet totally in the dark as to what I was *able* to do. Without language, training and money the prospects were very bleak. My wife Lily worked in a bakery in the West End; that was our only source of income.

A friend of my family gave me twenty pounds (a lot of money in those days), with the proviso that I should *write down* as much as I could remember about my past aspirations, hopes and dreams of the future. He said that I should not think whether what I wanted to do was realistic or not; just write it down. Afterwards, he said, we would see what the *real* possibilities were. (This man was not in the field of psychology but was a successful, hard-headed businessman.) I did what he suggested, and two weeks later I appeared at his office with my notes. What emerged from my introspection was important and useful to me, as in the continuous turmoil of my life I had had no real chance to look at myself closely.

As a child I had been very interested in what people were doing. Like most children, I suppose, I had an ability to observe details and atmosphere – an ability that adults unlearn in the process of growing up. I particularly used to notice whether people were bored or enthusiastic about what they were doing. Small as I was, I asked my mother what she thought about people who did not like what they were doing, and why adults 'did not play any more'. She answered me, 'People who don't like what they are doing are usually not very good at it', and, 'Adults have forgotten how to play: that's the problem.'

In my notes to our friend the recollection of such memories played a very important part, as I recalled that it had been my intention to become a 'playing adult' when I grew up.

As I dug deep into my early life, two aspects began to emerge: my real interest in people, and my wish somehow to write and document this interest. Translating these into the realm of possibilities in the late 1940s, what emerged was that I wanted to become some kind of psychologist and writer. Once this became clear, with effort, improved English, determination and Lily's help, I embarked on a journey to achieve both. I have never regretted my choices, and I have been grateful ever since to our friend who helped me to find the time and finance for my exploration. By the end of 1953 I had qualified as a psychiatric social worker at Manchester University, and had written several books, published here and abroad.

I hope that you, the reader, will see in this book that in order to become a 'playing adult' we need to search for our buried dreams. We need to unearth them, examine them and then fit them into the possibilities of reality. By *dreams* I mean that you need to assess in clear and understandable ways what your gifts are, and what your early aspirations were; and then, only then, you need to make a *plan*. You will, I hope, note that our gifts do not come only from our positive experiences but, just like in my own example, from painful 'negative' ones too.

This book will look at the *whole person*, with special emphasis on work, stagnation and unemployment. I shall show how personal frustration has the potential to be turned round so that it can lead to a more personally satisfying life.

# 1 'Help Means to Activate the Wish for Self-Help'

In times of unemployment, redundancy, or meaningless and repetitive work, we find ourselves wandering into a no-man's-land. Here we face fear, anxiety, worry, sometimes strange physical symptoms without obvious organic cause. Many of us may have times when we feel out of balance or emotionally upset. Problems, the struggles of everyday life, unhappiness and disappointments, create stress until we feel we can no longer cope. At such times we cannot simply 'pull ourselves together', and we are at a loss to know how to get ourselves out of our misery.

Usually the past, the present and the future merge into each other gently and slowly, so we have time, chance and opportunity to get used to the changes and prepare ourselves for them. But in the last two decades the changes have accelerated to the point where we no longer know what is happening to us. We know where we come from; we know the set patterns of our existence so far; but millions of men and women who are unemployed do not know where they are now, nor do they know where they are going. And those who are employed often do not know any more than the unemployed what will be expected of them, because new technology demands constant adaptations and changes. As a result of this, thousands of men and women are threatened with being thrown on the rubbish heap of society. It seems that neither Governments nor industry, commerce nor Trades Union, are as yet able to cope with these dramatic and drastic changes. The pattern of 'societal coping' is as much in a no-man's-land as is the individual. Policy and politics are hypnotised by what *was*, and thus close their eyes to

the needs of people, to their innate human potential, to their
dreams and aspirations; in fact the policy is to discourage
human beings from feeling useful, able and creative. *We pay
people to remain inactive.*

In such times, it is more important than ever before to be able
to understand what our human needs really are, what we
human beings are about, and to recognise too that these periods
of social and emotional change can be turned to our advantage,
enabling us to make more of our lives. Instead of feeling para-
lysed and impotent by the existence of such problems, and
instead of pretending that, since some of us may never suffer
from them, it does not matter if millions do, we must *all* learn
from the pains of this age and find out how to profit from them.
If we allow this learning process to take place, we will achieve a
deeper understanding of our needs and the needs of others. We
may or may not be able to find another 'job' in the traditional
sense, we may or may not be able to change our work if it does
not suit, but we can develop a different, less strained attitude to
life, to work and – I use the term for the first time – 'life task'. By
'life task' I mean the new pattern that may, for millions of
people, replace work itself.* As we search for understanding
and answers we must realise the following:-

1    The changes that have occurred and are occurring are
nobody's *fault*.

2    That Government, industry and Trades Unions have not
been used to looking at the emotional needs of people, but
rather concentrated on physical and financial needs. In 1955,
in an article, I concluded by saying the following:

> The Welfare State provides many forms of assistance
> besides financial help for those who are in need of it. All
> these are most important, but should not be considered the
> final answer to our social problems. The situation is some-
> what similar to that of a home where the material needs

* See also p. 112 below.

are provided for the child, but where, for various reasons, his emotional needs are not fully met. We have learnt a great deal about mental illness and emotional disturbance in the last thirty years, and the Welfare State should now see that, besides the many existing services, it should also make provision for the emotional needs of people who find it necessary to apply for National Assistance.*

3   That the educational system has not been geared to prepare young men and women for unemployment and now, moving towards the twenty-first century, we must re-think what education is really for.

Crisis, however, can equal potential. It does not simply mean that we will be defeated by events, but that we will turn the negative trends to our advantage. And so Goverment, industry, Trades Unions and the educational system must focus on the *individual*, his and her needs and the kind of help they need in this changing age.

As I said in the Introduction, for years I have been working with people who had considerable emotional and social problems, mainly as a result of unemployment, redundancy and stagnation. I found that people were very ambivalent about help. The lost, the frustrated, the childish part of their personality wanted me to do things for them. 'Help me' meant in this sense, 'Be a mother to me', remove discomfort, make me happy. But their adult self deeply resented this kind of 'help'. *The adult wanted to be able to solve his or her own problems*, but did not know how to go about it. It was in this latter area that the wish for self-help arose. And it was here, eventually, that I found methods, techniques, and a philosophy to assist people to regain or find mastery over their own lives. I realised that my job was not to do things *for* people, to advise them or tell them what was right or wrong with them, but rather to create some framework in which they could do things for themselves, have access

* Eugene Heimler, 'Psychiatric Socialwork with National Assistance Board Cases', *The Medical Officer*, 16 December 1955 (94, 351-353)

to their *own* source of knowledge, so that they could become their *own* psychological and social adviser. Only unhappy people choose to remain helplessly childish. Adults want to move on and leave the nursery behind. My task, therefore, was to allow them to experience the adult in themselves, even when they were feeling weak, and so enable them to grow away from dependency towards independence. But how does one help people to experience their adult self? Where does independence come from?

Many years ago I had a client who at the age of 45 lost a leg in an accident. He was in hospital for a long time, and then he had to learn how to use an artificial leg; finally he returned home, brooding about his misfortune. He became increasingly anxious and withdrawn, for he felt that he had no future. His wife also became very depressed as she saw this once very active man become morose and chair-bound. And the children, too, began to show signs of stress in school. Financially he just about managed, for he had received some compensation, but he *felt* that in time he and his family would be starving. He had been a builder, but there was no chance of his going back to do that.

His doctor called me to see if I could help him in any way. I soon realised that this man's problem could not be solved by any practical suggestion about training for a new job. First he had to take stock of his life and assess the implications of his accident. Before he could face life without his leg, he had to learn mentally to come to terms with what it meant. So I sat there and listened to him, for I felt that it was most important that he should be able to express whatever was on his mind. I became a *witness to his pain*. But not just the pain. As time went on, he began to speak about his past, about the fun he had had both as a child and as an adult. He usually finished on a bitter note, referring to the accident as the end of everything. Now and then I would say that this cannot be the end of everything, but he seemed not to hear me. Whatever I said, whatever opinion I offered, he dismissed it outright. And slowly it dawned on me that he was right. After all, it was he who had to live without a leg; I had no experience of it, so why should he trust my optimistic enthusiasm?

Then one day he spoke again about his misfortune and about the good times that he had had. I did not quite understand what he was saying, for I did not follow the connection between the past and the present, so I asked for some clarification. I repeated back to him some of the points he had just made, indicating at the end what was not clear to me. His answer surprised me. He did not offer me an explanation of the points I had raised, but he became rather thoughtful at the way I had *mirrored* back to him some of his own ideas. It seemed that he was in a different mood when he received back a summary at the conclusion of what he was saying than while he was talking. From then on I listened to him with 'a third ear'. I no longer tried to think of solutions or even that I should understand everything that he had said, nor did I keep trying to have suitable feelings towards him and his problems. Instead I simply listened. (Did I say simply? It was not that simple!) For no other reason than that he should understand himself. And whether I understood him or not, I tried to replay to him the essence of my understanding, to which the reaction was always the same: he became very thoughtful indeed.

He would become pensive about my playback and make some comments like 'Did I really say that?' or 'I said that, but what I really meant was. . .' I also noticed that our relationship had slowly changed. He became more and more intimate as I conveyed to him my understanding of what he was saying. I think he appreciated my effort to mirror back to him the essence of what he was feeling and thinking, and most of all he appreciated my *human concern*. He felt that I must respect him a great deal if I took so much notice of what he was saying and went to such lengths to understand him. Through this he began to see his life in a different light, in which the accident, however disabling, was only an episode in time. He began to see that he could have a future, and began to talk about what he could do, how he could use some of the compensation money to create a new livelihood. Helping him all the time to clarify his mind in the way I have described, by mirroring back to him what he actually said, I encouraged him to be more positive in his ideas until he eventually decided to buy a van, adapted to his special needs, and earn a living delivering groceries. He was once more self-supporting.

I saw him from time to time and he often spoke of our long conversations. Once he said to me: 'You know, you really did help me a lot, for you allowed me to sort things out.' *Allowing people to sort things out is the key. Help means to activate the wish for self-help.*

Over the years I realised that the greatest help I could offer to people who had work problems or some emotional problems was to listen to them. You may well say that anyone could listen, and what is so important about listening anyway? But listening in the way I describe can only be learnt through practice and time. Listening does not mean to lend an ear to someone. First we must have cleared our minds of prejudice, of our own thoughts and the wish to give advice. Listening with this kind of understanding helps a man or woman in pain, in confusion, or in problems with his or her work situation, to feel that he or she is at least not alone any more. Words cannot convey it enough. Listening carefully enabled me to understand the *meaning* of what was communicated. People in great anxiety like unemployment, redundancy or being stuck in an uncongenial job often feel that they are 'going out of their minds', that what they are saying makes no sense. Once they realise that it does make sense, they are helped to feel less insecure, less frantic. The fact that their human experience makes sense also confirms the validity of such an experience. However painful the experience may be, put together with other experiences *it does make sense*, and this can only come about by an appropriate, disciplined, psycho-social feed-back system.

This 'making sense' strengthens the individual so that he feels less tangled, cut off, less weak and childish and more independent. Earlier I asked the question where does independence come from. It comes from the recognition that we are capable of thought and action on our own: that we have sufficient trust in ourselves *to act.*

Whether problems are actual unemployment or stagnation in a given job, the effect is felt in other areas of life too. With the man who lost his leg there were considerable problems, as I mentioned, with his wife being depressed and the children having difficulties in school. When he was able to regain his self-respect and began his own choice of work and felt *able* to carry it through, there was eventually quite a remarkable change in the other members of the family too. I remember that when, in the 1950s, sudden unemployment hit some miners (which problem, unfortunately, still threatens many today) there was for a while a temporary sexual impotence, due to depression, in some of those people who became redundant and felt useless. I often said in my lectures that this was the first time in my experience that I clearly saw how changes in society can affect the most intimate areas of private lives. Their wives were often quite bewildered at how the changes affected their husbands. They had lived their lives according to a certain rhythm and pattern, an often satisfying pattern, and now they were quite unable to put into words what was going on. These women felt strongly that they wanted to stand by their men, and they did. But they could not understand why they turned away from them. When, after a while, the miners had found alternative work and their own depression lifted and their sexuality became normal again, the women found it very difficult to readjust themselves now to this change. So understanding ourselves and others is really of great value, whether we are miners, factory workers, office workers, professional people or whatever. Society, too, has got to understand the implications of purposeless activity.

Another example: a 40 year-old woman came to see me, bitterly unhappy about her husband, her children and her job. She felt that nothing had gone right for her, either in the past or in the present, and she blamed it all on her mother who, she felt, had never understood her. As I listened to her, played back her thoughts and feelings, and discussed alternative possibilities with her, she gradually seemed able to understand herself better, and decided to change her job. Eventually she found that the new environment suited her extremely well. Many of her problems still remained, but on the whole she had made her existence more satisfying. One day she spoke of her past with much less bitterness. I enquired how she had come round to this better view of her own childhood and her mother and she explained: 'When I last spoke to you about my mother I could only see the worst aspect of our relationship because I was feeling so bitter; but now that I feel more relaxed, I can look back and remember that there were good times too. My mother's own life must have been hard, and I can see now why she was so often unreasonable.'

Here is a good example of how, in times of personal loss, confusion and anxiety, one picks on what I call a 'scapegoat of past ghosts'. Inundated with problems, this woman had felt helpless and angry, totally frustrated and swamped, and had blindly attached all her problems onto one cause: Mother. But as she sorted out her tangled feelings in the present, mainly about her work problems, she felt more independent and her mother became less relevant. She learned to view her past in a new light and to see that she could do something to help herself, that it was possible to feel differently towards the past when one can do much more positive action in the present. *So deep feelings of resentment changed as a result of action in the present.*

Past and present are connected, and attitudes can be changed. Feelings about the past are not absolute. *They do not present final truth for all time, but are subjective temporary perceptions, dependent upon the experiences of the present.*

Often work problems are so mixed up with relationships, past and present, that we do not know what is wrong. Human experiences are very subjective, not only in terms of past/present: present/past, but also of what we are seeing, feeling, smelling, touching in our environment.

Take two people who go to the seaside together; one enjoys himself, the other feels bored and dejected. Both feel that everyone around them must share their mood. But we know that this is not true. Each also wishes to impose his own mood onto the other. We all know how aggravating that can be. So it is particularly important not to impose one's own moods, feelings and attitudes onto other people. If I can replay to someone what I hear, then my hope is that he or she will hear him or herself, and thus the meaning of the experience will become much clearer.

A 32 year-old man came with a problem which he faced daily at his work:

> I am responsible for a number of people and my boss expects them to produce more and more. He does not seem to realise that they are having a raw deal and that the poor bastards are working to their limits. He won't accept this, but calls them lazy and says that I am soft in the head. I tell him that we have got to employ more people, but he just does not want to know and never even listens. I start to say a few words and he just blasts off at me. He never listens to me. He is getting on my nerves. I feel like saying to him: 'You bloody bastard, stop and listen!' Yesterday I blew up and told him what I thought of him. To my surprise he was not angry, just looked hurt and said; 'Joe, don't you understand, I am being pushed much more than you are, don't you realise the pressures on me?' I was furious. 'You and your pressures. It is my men who are being pushed about and pressurised.'

When he stopped in his narrative I used this sudden silence to say to him: 'Let me try to put to you what you have just told me, and see if I understood you. Correct me if what I say is not what you said. I understood you saying that your boss does not realise how much he is pressurising your men. He thinks that they are lazy.' Joe interrupted: 'Well, he did not actually say "lazy" although it all came out like that.' I went on: 'You say that he did not say that they were lazy but that it all came out like that.'

| | |
|---|---|
| JOE: | It sounds funny to hear you saying it like that. |
| ME: | What is so funny? |
| JOE: | That he did not say it, but that I said that he did. (*Silence.*) |
| ME: | You also said that your boss never listens to you. |
| JOE: | Well, he bloody well never listens to anyone and that is the truth. |
| ME: | Eventually you blew up and told him what you thought of him, to which he said that you did not understand the pressures he was under, that you could not see that because you were thinking only of your men. (*Silence.*) |
| JOE: | He may be under pressure, I don't know. |
| ME: | What do you mean? |
| JOE: | If he is under pressure and tells me so, why don't I find out whether it is true or not? |
| ME: | Well, why don't you? (*After a long silence.*) |
| JOE: | Because I had not thought of his point of view up to now and now I'll have to, won't I? I really have to find out what he is talking about. |

So the boss had not actually used the word 'lazy', but Joe's subjective understanding was that he had. He had not even noticed this until he heard it from me. Then when he did notice it he found it 'funny'. He had not been in the least concerned about the boss before, but towards the end of my summary he became interested in him and understood him better.

We have such a great need to communicate ourselves to others, and somehow we have forgotten how to do this. And we have lost the ability to notice other people's need to communicate to us. I say 'forgotten', for as children we were very well aware of these needs. As adults, all too many of us have not only forgotten the art of direct, uncomplicated ways of communication, but we have even lost the art of observing the world around us. Much of this world has become dead.

As a child I remember how the streets and gardens used to give out a curious odour after rain. How I used to inhale the fragrance of fresh dough in a bakery. The world was full of magic and mystery then, and, alas, adulthood has washed away the original excitement of seeing the world in such a lively way.

Can we regain our old wonder and the sharpness of primary observation? Yes, I think so. We must discover within ourselves the spontaneity of listening and talking. Many people today have to pay for a listener. Our society has created an enormous market for professional listeners, partly because no one else listens to us any more. Friends are ready with quick advice that is based on *their* experience and not on our own. Husbands and wives develop methods of 'selective listening'. They only take notice of what concerns them. Increasingly we feel cut off, alienated and lonely, even when we are surrounded by people.

So the first step in helping yourself to overcome frustrations and problems in your life is to learn how to listen. And when you have learned how to listen and how to understand others, you will be better equipped to apply this ability to yourself and to hear yourself. And when you have learned how to hear yourself, you will begin to understand how to isolate your real problems from the general confusion of your life. Once you have come to terms with the root cause of your difficulties, you must take stock of each and every aspect of your life, and see what positive action you could take. By positive action I mean that certain decisions have to be carried out. This positive action more often than not will be in the area of what I call 'life tasks' (see page 112). If we can find meaning in our lives we should be able to put right many often seemingly complicated inter-personal problems.

At the beginning of this chapter I spoke about a no-man's-land where in time of crisis we often wander, not knowing which way to turn. I gave you some examples of people who found themselves in this no-man's-land, and eventually they were able not only to leave it, but to move towards a new existence. And I said that the key to finding the way is in two directions. First, in trying to listen and understand others and ourselves, and then to formulate a plan which must be concrete, workable and satisfying. Now that does not mean that those of us who are unemployed today will find employment tomorrow. But it may mean that today we begin to think about what alternatives there are in our lives to find some meaning which may lead, if not to an employment, to a more satisfying existence, and also perhaps eventually earning our livelihood. It does not mean that we have to leave that job that we hate so much, but we have to find, *somewhere* in our life, some meaningful task which is satisfying and makes the other, the job, bearable. These are small beginnings, and alone, without support, may be difficult to achieve. But not at all impossible.

In the next chapter I will speak about active listening, a process which was helpful to me at a time when I was un-employed, and which later helped many others.

# 2 Active Listening to Others and Oneself

All people have problems and all people have crises. These, however, do not often warrant a psychiatrist or analyst or therapist, provided you, the reader, have a framework in which to do self-explorations and the know-how which I will now describe. No other qualifications are needed, other than a wish to overcome your problems, a respect for your own past experience and a certain amount of self-discipline and perseverance. Problems that weigh on us do not usually appear overnight; even if it appears that they do, they have a long story reaching back to your yesterdays. So do not expect immediate results, but, with hard work, self-healing can happen. You also need an ability for observation. As self-observation is the route to recovery and success, you will need to practise the art of observation first. When I say practice I do not mean that you have to work hard at it, but rather to sharpen your awareness about people and objects.

Let me give you as an example the following extract from a conversation; after you have read it I would like you to write down as briefly as possible what you think the speakers are like and what you feel are their problems.

She was 31 and he was 36 years old. The woman was a divorcee, the man married with two children. Both joined a drama society. The conversation took place in the coffee break.

MAN: Tonight wasn't particularly good; it was too slow for my liking.

WOMAN: Oh I don't know; I suppose it must go up and down. Acting can't be perfect all the time. If anything the play itself is slow.

MAN:      I don't know about you, but I hate it when things drag on. I need action; what is life without action? Boring!

WOMAN:   But it can't be action all the time. There must be periods of peace and tranquillity; periods when one can be alone. Don't you like to be alone?

MAN:      I hate it. I get restless and don't know what to do with myself. I don't even enjoy watching TV alone. I need to have people around me.

WOMAN:   Any people?

MAN:      I think. . . I mean people. They don't have to be close friends or anything like that as long as they're on your wavelength.

WOMAN:   And what is that?

MAN:      What is what?

WOMAN:   You said 'wavelength'.

MAN:      I meant as long as you can talk to each other.

WOMAN:   I see. But I can't enjoy just talking. I must know the people first.

MAN:      How will you know them if you don't give them a chance?

WOMAN:   That's true. That's the story of my life. I don't often give people a chance. I've become distrustful I suppose.

MAN:      How come?

WOMAN:   Oh it's a long story which would bore you.

MAN:      I'm not bored.

WOMAN:   No, only I would rather not go into it.

MAN:      (*After some silence.*) You turn off when it gets hot, don't you?

WOMAN:   Yes, I suppose so.

*          *          *

Have you made your observations? If so, let me see if they are similar to mine.

The man says he needs constant stimulation. Without action, life, to him, is boring. He cannot bear to be alone; anyone will do for company, but he must have someone. Yet he is quite observant and, given the chance, is willing to listen. She, on the other hand, appears cautious and contemplative. She says that she must know people well to be comfortable with them. Her problem is that she does not give them a chance, as she is not giving him a chance to get to know her. (Is she avoiding talking about herself because she is afraid of being hurt?) To sum up, he appears superficial but capable of depth. She appears to have some depth but to be incapable of showing it.

What I have done in the first instance is not to form an opinion of these two people, but to *extract* from each what they have said. Only then did I form a picture of both.

Try to listen to people with the view that you will, at an appropriate point in time, mirror back to them what they have been saying. You will notice not only your increased ability in observation, but also their deepest gratitude. They will be grateful, first, because you have listened to everything they said, and, secondly, because you listened so thoroughly that you remembered what they were saying. You will help them more doing this than with any amount of advice you may give them. This mirroring back process allows them to reflect on what they were saying and bring their experiences into focus. You will find that you, too, learn a great deal, more than if you stepped in with advice too soon. If you did not understand something, naturally you can ask, but when you ask be sure you don't break their train of thought. Using this 'technique' you will find that friends will talk to you much more, and with greater fluency, and they will respond better. This same approach can become an invaluable asset in work too. Before you move on to express an opinion or give advice, it helps to sum up all you have learned so far. This, too, is very reassuring to people and encourages them to feel that they have been understood. Here is an example:

BOB:    I don't feel as self-confident as I used to. I've been selling this product for years, yet lately my sales figures have dropped; I think it's because my heart's no longer in the business. I don't know why, or when it started, but I am afraid that I'm not getting through to the buyers any more; in fact I know I'm not. Each call is becoming a nightmare; I feel funny in my head and I feel my stomach tightening up all the time. I'm worried. After all, my livelihood is at stake.

ME:     Let me see if I've understood you. You were saying that lately, for reasons unknown to you, you've lost your self-confidence and now you feel physically ill during your calls. You are afraid and you don't feel you are getting through.

BOB:    Yes. What you said is correct except, come to think of it, I think I do know some of the reasons . . . (*Silence.*)

ME:     Tell me, Bob, what are your reasons?

BOB:    It's very personal. It is not only in my work that I doubt myself. It's everywhere. At home with Joan . . .
(*Silence again*)

ME:     What about Joan?

BOB:    You know, the kids play her up during the day and by the time I get home she's all worked up; then she takes it out on me, nag nag nag. Now I know that Joan doesn't mean to be like that, but she is. Just when I feel like a quiet evening with her, she ruins the atmosphere; then I freeze up and I can't talk. Then I get angry with her and I know I shouldn't be. It's all very confusing.

ME:     So one reason why you've lost confidence lately is that Joan is so tired out by the end of the day that she can't give you the attention and affection you need.

BOB: That's right, but what can I do about it? What do you think?

ME: Let's try to see what you could do about it.

BOB: She needs to be free from the children, but how?

ME: Let's think about it. How could you help her?

BOB: I personally can't. Baby sitting is only a partial answer. I feel we ought to go away for a few days and find each other again. After all, we still love each other.

ME: So love is still there and you need to go away without the children.

BOB: I'm sure that's right. My mother would be only too glad to have them for a weekend, then we could go away and plan things out better.

ME: But tell me, Bob, how will this help you with your job?

BOB: Well . . . we haven't been . . . intimate for some time; perhaps being together like that would give me back some of my lost self-confidence.

ME: So you see a connection between your lost confidence at work and your problems with Joan?

BOB: Yes, it hasn't been so clear to me before as it is now, but that seems to be it.

It would have been only too easy to take up Bob's point about his work difficulties, to reassure him by giving him advice. But then we would not have covered very important areas in Bob's life which were a contributing factor to his loss of interest and confidence. In that case the conversation might have gone something like this:

BOB: I don't feel as self-confident as I used to. I've been selling this product for years, yet lately my sales figures have dropped because my heart's not in the business any more.

ME: Oh that's too bad, Bob.

BOB: So you think too that it's bad.

ME:     Well it's not good, is it! Why do you think things aren't going too well for you at the moment?

BOB:    (*Now on guard*) I don't really know.

ME:     Oh, it may be just a passing phase; do you remember that I went through a bad patch some years ago but eventually it was OK? You will do the same – I'm sure you will.

BOB:    I hope so.

ME:     Would you care for a drink?

\*          \*          \*

And that would have been that. I would have left him with his problems unsolved, giving him the impression, quite rightly, that I didn't care that much. Or I might have listened further and then expressed concern about the funny feelings he had in his head and stomach, perhaps advising him to see a doctor.

With active listening this becomes irrelevant. What is relevant is that he should open up, begin to look at his own life objectively, try to crystallise his problem and then start to think of some action he could take.

These exercises in awareness will ultimately help not only others, but you personally. You will find out how hard it is for people to see their lives *as a whole* and how preoccupied they become with one facet only, especially a facet that is not going well. You will recognise how difficult it is for people to 'step outside themselves' and become their own observer. This knowledge will help you later, when you are alone without a sounding board and you have to face and solve many of your own problems. The route to self-discovery, paradoxically, starts with others. Apart from your giving others feed-back, you will also develop an increasing sense of perception; in other words a recognition and realisation of the kind of feelings that you are experiencing. These feelings will vary immensely from good to violent, but whatever they may be you must allow them recognition and acceptance, for later on these feelings can be looked at and their messages deciphered. Feelings are our warning system; the more you are 'in touch' with them, the more they will teach you about yourself. You will find that you may have been ignoring many of them. Had you been able to 'listen' to them more carefully, you might have acted very differently in many of the difficult situations in your life.

In order to explain this I would now like to return to my conversation with Bob, and so share with you what I thought and felt at the time, and then I will try to decipher some of these thoughts and feelings. I must remind you that my feelings are subjective and they only serve here as a demonstration of the process I have been describing. You, naturally, would have other feelings, no more or less relevant than my own.

| | |
|---|---|
| BOB: | I don't feel as self-confident as I used to. |
| (*My reaction*): | Some slight feeling of anxiety, as if Bob were expressing something I too had personally experienced. I feel I would like to reach out to reassure him (or to reassure myself). |
| | A vague picture passes through my mind. Some years ago I had to go before a Selection Board for an important job. When I entered the room I was aware of an impersonal atmosphere. Six or seven men and women sat there like jurors. I felt as if I had committed some crime. I tried to smile but there was no response. My confidence ran into my knees and I felt them start to shake. |

BOB: I've been selling this product for years, yet lately my sales figures have dropped; I think it's because my heart's no longer in the business.

(*My reaction*): When was it – four or five years ago? I too felt very gloomy. I feel that same sense of gloom now. Everything seems pointless. I am also unreasonably angry with Bob for reviving my own old unpleasant feelings. I don't want to be reminded of my own times of misery.

BOB: I don't know why, or when it started, but I am afraid that I'm not getting through to the buyers any more; in fact I know I'm not.

(*My reaction*): For a second I see Bob in a glass cage. He is shouting something but I can't hear him. Then I am in the glass cage with him. I want to scream out but no voice is coming out of my throat. Auschwitz! The electrified wires are surrounding the camp; there is no way out.

BOB: Each call is becoming a nightmare.

(*My reaction*): I want to say to him: 'Yes, Bob, I know.'

BOB: I feel funny in my head and I feel my stomach tightening up all the time. I'm worried. After all, my livelihood is at stake.

(*My reaction*): Why can't he get himself out of this? I feel angry. A grown man shouldn't feel so helpless. If I faced those bloody buyers. . . Images: my father is hitting me, I don't know what I've done. I am completely at his mercy. He is big and strong and I am small and weak.

As Bob keeps on talking, all kinds of feelings and thoughts

flash through my mind. If I allow them to break into consciousness they do, and they tell me something relevant about *me*. Messages speak about *my* insecurity, *my* struggles, *my* depression and anger. If I open up while Bob is speaking I can experience myself through him.

*The first step towards self-discovery is to be able to experience oneself through others.*

Another way of experiencing yourself through others is by selecting out those comments in other people's conversations which strike you as being significant the next day. Develop your memory and try to remember as much as you can about what was said in conversation with someone the day before. Whatever you select out from the talk will be significant, for whatever comes to mind most readily will be relevant to you personally. Then try to discover why you have remembered that particular phrase, and then endeavour to express its relevance to yourself. Through *selective remembering* you will learn more about yourself as well as more about the other person.

If I think back to my own conversation with Bob, what comes to mind first is his feeling 'funny in the head', his giddiness, although at the time I didn't take much notice of this point; now that I realise that I have selected this memory before all others, I remember the feeling of vertigo that I too used to get in tense situations. When I was in Auschwitz they mixed bromide in our food, which made us feel dizzy and giddy. Later on in life, faced with situations that I disliked, I used to experience somewhat similar feelings. It took me quite a long time to get over these feelings, but the first time I understood why I had them and where they came from their effect was less frightening. And so it may be with you. If through listening to the problems of others you can spot similar difficulties of your own, or can work out the reasons for some of your more bizarre feelings or the origin of some odd sensation, then you are starting to know more about yourself.

To sum up:

Listen
Observe
Recapitulate
Crystallise
Remember

The first step towards self-discovery consists of active listening. Then learn how to give back the essence of what has been said to you in order to help the other person to begin to sort himself out. During this process, however, you will experience many personal feelings. Because of the context in which they were raised, you may see them in a new light, and so gain greater insight into yourself at the same time. Try to learn from all the feelings and thoughts that this active listening has aroused. This in turn will make you more observant, more self-aware and more self-objective.

Now do the same thing for yourself. If you can borrow a tape recorder it is easier and quicker, but if not, take a pencil and paper and write down your own thoughts, however confusing they may appear. Having done this (or talked into the machine) read them through (play back). Observe and think over what you have said. Mirror back to yourself in a shortened form what you have just written down or said. Is that what you meant? Is that what you meant to say? Listen to yourself again as you play it all back. Are you explaining your true feelings? Try to synthesise what you are saying in the pithiest way possible, crystallise the nugget of your thoughts into two or three simple sentences. Continue to do this until you feel that you are reaching the heart of the matter.

Learn how to listen so that you can recognise your own pattern of responses, your own particular problems, frustrations and satisfactions. Find out what matters to you.

Having identified your problems in this way you should then become much clearer, not only about where your difficulties lie, but also about the positive steps that you can take in order to change your situation. This positive action, even the planning of it, should help you a great deal to modify your feeling of frustration. But – you must learn to listen creatively: first to others, then to yourself.

# 3   Satisfactions and Frustrations in Balance

Early in my professional life I noticed that when people had emotional problems they were so hypnotised by them that, very often, they were unable to think about anything else. Preoccupied with their problems, they harped ceaselessly on the gloomy, negative sides of their lives, and paid little or no attention to the more satisfying aspects. They became blind to their past satisfactions too; the gloom of their immediate difficulties blinkered their vision, their whole view of life became lopsided. When I enquired about positive assets they would supply me with a list of these, but at the same time managed to convey that they were utterly unimportant. What *was* important was what they did *not* have. Because they denied themselves the positive aspects in their lives, they were unable to deal with the negative ones. In a true sense, their satisfactions and frustrations were completely out of balance. Satisfactions and frustrations have a great deal to do with the utilisation or otherwise of our potentials. A definition for satisfaction could be *the individual's subjective perception that he is making good use of his potentials*. And frustration can be defined as *the individual's subjective perception that he cannot make use of his potentials*. Now potentials are either given potentials or acquired potentials. Given are those potentials with which we are born; often we do not even realise that we have these because we take them for granted. The ability to breathe, to use one's arms or legs; these only become noticeable when we have some problems in breathing or in movement. The ability to use ourselves as fully as we can is also our potential. Acquired potentials are those that we learn as skills throughout life. Now it depends on the social system whether we can use our acquired potentials or not. In these days of serious unemployment many people cannot use their acquired potentials, because they have no way in which they can find an expression for them. So society has a great deal to do with the ability or inability to use our potentials.

I also observed that a certain amount of satisfaction was necessary in order to function fully in life. And, I may add, that a certain amount of frustration was also necessary in order to give the motivation for functioning. The balance, however, between satisfaction and frustration had to be right, because if the frustrations were overpoweringly great, then the individual's functioning was greatly affected. There also appeared to be a relationship between satisfactions and frustrations and their ratio to each other, and physical and emotional symptoms. Conversely, when people had a large number of frustrations and few satisfactions, and they were able to increase their satisfactions in time, such symptoms often disappeared. It therefore became very important to have an accurate assessment of perceived satisfaction and frustration, even to measure them in some way, so that in the first instance an accurate picture would emerge. What was very interesting to notice was that the subjective perception of satisfaction and frustration corresponded to the observation of others. In time I devised an instrument which goes under my name (The Heimler Scale of Social Functioning) which looked at certain patterns in each particular area of human life. This Scale had two purposes: to be able to establish an accurate picture of an individual's functioning, and to share this with the client. Another one is to be able to reflect on the questions through the answers given, and to make some sense of the answers. This Scale is very different from psychological tests because its primary use is not for the therapist, but for the client himself. Thorough training is needed to be able to use the Scale, and that takes time. However, I can share with you, the reader, certain aspects of my findings which are not as elaborate, detailed and precise as the Scale itself, and you will thus be able to gain a great deal of

knowledge and understanding about your own 'social functioning'. In this chapter I hope to give you some idea of how you
can do this and how you can come to some kind of assessment or
picture of yourself, and then how you move on from this newly-
gained knowledge towards some action in the areas where you
need further satisfaction.

As I mentioned earlier, another factor which appeared early
in my work was that a certain amount of frustration, not too
overwhelming, was necessary to succeed in life. The aim of
human life, therefore, is not to eliminate frustrations but rather
to use them. In this connection I must say that frustrations are
often the potential for satisfaction, because of the pressure they
put on us to do things which, if we were fully happy and
satisfied, we might not want to do.

Before I move on to the bare bones of the Scale itself, I need
just to say that if we find ourselves blindly blaming others for
everything that seems to be going wrong in our lives, if we feel
bad-tempered, anti-social, aggressive and defiant in turn, and
imagine outside events beyond our control, we need to pause for
a moment, sit back quietly and look carefully at our lives. Just
where do our difficulties lie? What exactly are our problems?
We also want to look at the compensating advantages of our
lives: where do we find our pleasures, our moments of happiness
and achievement? Why have we let our lives get so out of
balance? We cannot all be successful, nor can we all succeed at
everything we turn our hand to, but we can all accomplish
something, the achievement of which makes us feel happy.
Most of us gain our pleasures in small ways from a wide variety
of experiences: perhaps from listening to music or playing the
piano, however badly; from our relationships with friends,
children or parents; from gardening, some kind of hobby or
from sport; from a difficult task well done. Provided we have
enough moments in, say a week, which please us, and provided
these moments add up to more than the times at which we feel
fed up, then we are beginning to balance our lives adequately. If
the balance is upset, we must find out where it went wrong. We

must learn to assess ourselves, so that we know both where and when we have let frustrations outweigh pleasures. And we must learn how to redress this balance in ourselves.

It is my experience and conviction that however badly things are going in our lives, there are doors, which we need to find, through which we can enter into a more satisfying existence. I spoke in earlier chapters about the problems that so many people are facing today, those of unemployment, redundancy and stagnation. The search for answers, the search to be able to act on the answers, can make all the difference between living a life of emptiness and one of purpose. On my Scale there are five main areas of our lives from which all of us gain, or potentially can gain, satisfactions:

*1   Work and/or interest*

This occupies most of our waking hours and, as I have so often said, is of immense importance to us all. We need either work or some form of life task to keep our minds in balance, for inactivity is soul-destroying.

*2   Finance*

Money provides us with food and shelter, our everyday needs, and is also the source of many of our pleasures; lack of it can deny us so much.

*3   Friendship*

Not only those close friends with whom we share our lives, but friendship with people outside our intimate circle to talk to, with whom to share ourselves.

*4   Family*

Both family of origin, which gives our roots, and our own acquired family, which provides us with a sense of belonging, with love and with responsibility.

*5   Personal*

This includes the more intimate relationships like sexuality, which has a powerful effect on our feelings of success, emotional well-being, love and happiness. But sexuality cannot be, and must not be, isolated from our emotions and feelings, because on its own it has very little significance.

Not all these areas can be filled to the brim with a sense of satisfaction all the time. Some will have more than others. Some people may gain a great deal of happiness from one source and little from another. Many may miss out on one source altogether; but the wider the spread the better. If some satisfaction is gained from each section, then there are more choices open to the individual when he wants to increase his amount of pleasure and so feel that he is emotionally in balance. As you cannot fill these five areas to the brim (or only very seldom), there will always have to be a certain sense of frustration in all of us. This not only has to be tolerated but, as I said earlier, acts as a spur, and therefore appears to be essential. Indeed it becomes a spur to challenge us to action. It is the driving force which stimulates and enlivens us towards overcoming difficulties, gives us our sense of achievement. This is why frustration can be a potential for satisfaction, provided we understand clearly *what it is* that frustrates us. What we do not want to do, however, is to let a series of *impressions* rule our lives and believe that these impressions represent reality.

Let me take the various life areas again:-

1   Work
2   Finance
3   Friendship
4   Family
5   Personal

Put these questions in front of you and ask yourself, for example: 'How far am I satisfied with my work or interest?' If the answer is an unqualified 'yes', give 20 points for it. If your answer reflects any uncertainty, give 10. And if your answer is 'no' give 0. Thus the maximum possible score on this very simple system (if I can call it a system in this form) would be 100 and the minimum would be 0. Do the same with the other life areas, always starting with the question: 'How far am I satisfied with my financial situation, friendships, family and the personal/sexual aspects of my life?' If you score anything between 0 and 30, you will find that you are carrying, for the moment, a burden which has to be lifted. You may even feel that life is really overwhelmingly upsetting. In this case, I think we all need some help to sort ourselves out; and it may be that the self sorting-out may be somewhat difficult – but not impossible. If the scores are between 30 and 60, that indicates that we need to look very carefully at our resources, alone or with some help, to try to sort out which way we can realistically go. (And I assure you that in my experience there is more often than not *some* possibility open to us.) The norm – that is, the score in which you would feel in balance – would be around 70, in which case your life is probably functioning fairly well and in balance between satisfaction and frustration.

You must realise that this very simple scheme is just that: *a simple attempt to evaluate where we are.*

This is *not* my Scale of Social Functioning; that has many more questions and its scoring is somewhat different and more precise. What I am trying to give you here is some simple guidance to find where you stand and, possibly, which way you may need to go. This particular simple assessment between 0 and 100 is, of course, not scientific; nevertheless, when I started to develop my Scale, I worked with these very simple areas and they worked for me as well as later for others. It was the foundation of my Scale which was fully researched and tested. Before, however, you begin to score your life areas, be clear on what you are aiming for.

It is very important, of course, to fill one's life with *available* satisfactions so that the frustrations are kept within manageable limits. There will be times, of course, even in the lives of 'normal' people, when temporary upsets occur. If you know that you are more vulnerable during these times of temporary upheavals, you can help yourself to survive such a crisis by creating better opportunities to feel satisfied in another part of your life. Temporary frustrations are often normal – prolonged massive frustrations are not.

I referred earlier to the fact that frustrations are the potential for satisfactions. This, of course, can only be true if the frustrations are not overwhelming. When they are, then you need to reduce the frustration level by any means possible to a manageable level.

In order to change our frustrations into satisfactions, I said earlier, we need to understand ourselves. Action for change begins with self-knowledge. There are some obvious things which we should always know: our likes and dislikes, particularly in relation to our needs. 'I like my job a lot', or, 'in certain situations of financial stress I feel tension', are not enough. It is important to understand *what* I like about my job, *how* financial insecurity triggers off feelings of stress. We need not go through these processes all the time and become very introspective, but we should do so sometimes at least, when we need to sort things out, so that we become more knowledgeable about ourselves. In a sense we are preparing ourselves for self-help at a time when problems do occur, especially if these are connected with important decisions that we have to make.

So the process will begin by your evaluating the five areas – work, finance, friendship, family and personal areas – on the simple point system. When the scores are clear, then the next step will be to look at each area and put down some facts about each. So now take pencil and paper (or tape recorder) and examine and assess the five main areas of your life.

### 1   Work
Evaluate the positive and negative aspects of your work. Put down on paper the satisfactions and the frustrations that you experience there, and then examine what you have written down. Sum up your conclusions and take out what you find is most significant or relevant. When you have done this, think about your work area and score for yourself according to my

earlier suggestion of 20 for a completely satisfied 'yes' answer, 10 for uncertain or 'perhaps' answers, or partial satisfactions, and 0 for no satisfactions at all. After you have evaluated and expressed in writing (or with the help of a tape recorder) your basic satisfactions and frustrations in the area of work, score 20, 10 or 0. To give you an example:

A 44 year-old accountant writes:

I like my contact with people. Behind the figures of tax returns there are human lives and this fascinates me. I do not like to do too much actual accounting in one stretch without the opportunity of meeting some of my clients in person. I find that without such contact the figures are totally meaningless. So actual 'accountancy' is of less interest to me than people. In fact, if I had to become a mere book keeper, I would climb up the wall. I like the fact that my work brings certain financial rewards. So what I like about my work is people, and what I dislike about my work is figures. The most important thing for me, therefore, is to maintain a balance between people and facts.

(My score in work is: 20)

## 2 *Finance*

When you have evaluated your work situation, you can now move on, in a similar fashion, to the financial area of your life. Think carefully what benefits money brings to your life and what difficulties you are experiencing. Sum up your conclusions and extract at the end the most significant points and then give yourself a score of 20, 10 or 0. Another example:

A 38 year-old woman, single, secretary to a high powered executive, writes:

Money gives me the opportunity to live a reasonably comfortable life, to go to concerts and to go for holidays. When I want to buy a book that I have read about or heard about, I can do so and the same applies to buying records and such things. Unfortunately, I have let money play a very important part in my life; perhaps as a reaction to the poverty that I experienced in my parents' home. In consequence I have put money before personal relationships and, in my younger days, I was rather choosy. So money, in fact, hurt my chances of getting married, which I now deeply regret.

Looking at what I have written down, it is clear to me that giving money such a priority in my life spoilt my chances of marrying; perhaps it is still not too late. Perhaps I ought to get my priorities right; *now*, after all, it should not be impossible to combine my financial freedom and my need for independence with a good relationship with a man.

(My score in finance is: 10)

### 3 *Friendship*

Next look at the area of friendship. What do you get out of friendship, what do you offer to your friends? Are there needs *in this area* that are not satisfied? Again examine these and take out the most significant aspects which are relevant to you.

A 51 year-old professional man writes:

As I get older I find that friendship is more and more important to me. Although I have an excellent relationship with my wife, I find that with a friend I can look even at my relationship with her in a different and more sober light. I think, all round, it helps me to be frank and to be understood. It is also important to me that I am not just the receiver but that I can also give similarly. I have had this friend, a man of my age, for many years. We practically grew up together, and I am also very interested to hear his life problems, and I am glad that, here and there, I have added to his decisions and clarity. I don't need to have close friendships with many people. Although I like people, I would consider only a very few on the same level that I described. What is not satisfied in this respect? I cannot say that anything is not satisfied. The giving and

taking, I feel, is almost therapeutic, and I use that word very carefully. I feel that everyone ought to have such relationships with someone. My friend and I do not meet that often, but the very fact that he exists, and *can* be available, is of enormous help.
(My friendship score is: 20)

## 4 Family

A. Your family of origin. Examine your childhood: what are the good and bad experiences that come to mind? When you have assessed these try to sum up and, again, take out the most important aspects. Note: irrespective of whether or not you are living with your family of origin, this area should be commented on. *However, if you live with your wife and children, i.e. you have a present family,* then you will actually *score* only your present family, only keeping in mind the information about your family of origin, so that you still have a complete picture of past and present.

A 27 year-old woman, a music teacher, writes:

As I look back I have a warm feeling towards my parents. Then the feeling changes to sadness because, after my father's death, when I was a child, things were never the same. When my mother married again I could never accept her husband as my father. So it seems, as I recall the events of my childhood, basically it is good, but I was deeply saddened by my father's death. I also realised that it was not my stepfather's fault that we were not close. He tried to get near to me; it was I who prevented any nearness. To sum up, I feel that those early warm feelings gave me a good start in life, and on the whole this is reflected in the good relationships that I have with people.
(My primary family score is: 10)

B. Your present family. If you are married, what are the satisfying and frustrating aspects of your relationship with your spouse? Also, how do you feel about your children: are the feelings basically good or not? Examine your feelings towards your wife/husband and towards your children. If you are not married, but live with someone who either has or has not children, provided you consider this ongoing relationship significant, you should score this area and add *this* score to the final score you will have. If, however, you feel that, though you have a relationship, it is not that important to you and your family of origin is still more important, then you should score your primary family; but still express your feelings about your present relationship, so that you have a complete picture of past and present. You may only *score* in one area in order to keep to a maximum of 100, otherwise your scores will be distorted and useless for your self-evaluation.

A 47 year-old married woman writes:

I can always rely on him (*meaning her husband*). Whenever I need him he is there. I married rather young and have not regretted marrying him. He has been a good husband and a good father. On the negative side, I do feel that, whilst totally reliable, emotionally he often does not click with me. This has also caused (and is still causing) me some problems in our sexual relationship. Whilst I love him very dearly, I wish he could be just that bit more sensitive. If I look at the whole picture, I cannot complain. Life does not give perfect answers.
(My secondary family score is: 10)

A 23 year-old engineer writes:

Frankly, I don't like being single. Although I am still young, I would like to settle down. I don't like living alone; I don't like eating alone, and I am getting a little bit tired of continuously going out to eat. I have had one or two girl friends, but somehow they were not the type I wanted to marry. My problem is that I don't know exactly what that 'type' is. Somehow I am afraid that she may never turn up;

so I am not that happy. In a way I am a bit scared of the future in this respect. Though I have no close relationship, I want to score this area which is more relevant to me than my primary family.

(Score: 0)

Many single men and women may feel that their single status, and not the primary family, should be scored. This is all right, provided the information on the primary family is also expressed, and, of course, *not* scored.

## 5  *Personal*

Now look at the personal areas of your life. What are the satisfactions in your very private, personal sexual relationship? What is and what is not fulfilled? Think carefully about this and be as honest with yourself as possible. Then sum it all up.

A 37 year-old musician writes:

I was married before, and my relationship with my wife was not good, I suppose. My problem is that I have satisfactory sexual experiences when I am not committed and these somehow turn sour in an ongoing relationship. As I do want to have a permanent relationship, I tend therefore to discount the pleasures I get from casual affairs. I want to understand where the fault lies. Was the failure of my first marriage just a coincidence or is something wrong with me? I may need some outside help with these problems.

(My score in my personal area is: 0)

Now once more may I briefly sum up what you finally add up and what you don't, in order to avoid all possible confusion. Everyone adds up their scores in the areas of work, finance, friendship and personal. Those who are single, and to whom the most relevant relationship is still the *original family*, will score the primary family. If, however, the most relevant relationship is in the present family (secondary family) or in a relationship of great significance, or simply that the single status without a relevant relationship is more significant than the primary family, do not score the primary family. **What you must not do is score and add up both primary and secondary family. If you do that you distort the picture of the total scores you have.**

Now let me give you one example, where the five areas are scored by one person so that you have some further guide lines.
    This is a 35 year-old unemployed teacher:

At the moment I am unemployed, and while I have tried to get jobs, so far I have not succeeded. I am still trying, but the question now becomes stronger and stronger whether I will get a job in the foreseeable future. At times I am quite desperate. I am questioning whether I should be doing something else and, if so, what?
(My work score is: 0)

   I have some savings, and I get some interest from a small inheritance, but this is not enough for me to live on. Naturally I also get unemployment benefit. I could turn my small savings into some small business but I don't know where to start. My financial situation, whilst not that rosy, is not as yet desperate.
(My financial score is: 10)

   I have had and still have some close friends, and they are a real source of strength to me. I meet them quite often and we speak very often about our situations, including my own predicament. They are still working and they are family men, while I am single, or rather divorced. The relationship with my few friends is very close and satisfying.
(My friendship score is: 20)

   My original family was very supportive and, in some great measure, still is, although as they live away from London I don't see them that often. I know that I can

always rely on them as I could in the past. I had a very happy and secure childhood and feel that without that I would not be as optimistic as I am now.
(My primary family score is: 20)

I was married, and my marriage unfortunately did not work out. I am also the father of a small girl whom unfortunately I do not see as often as I would like. My marriage was a disaster and contributed to a great extent to the fact that I am unemployed today. I cannot count this relationship as my primary relevance here because in fact it is not. I do have some relationships but they are casual and I do not think they would count as strongly as my first family. My secondary family score with these relationships, if I counted them, would not add up to much anyway.
(My secondary family: *not scored*)

Despite the fact that I do not have an ongoing relationship, my sexual relationship with women since my divorce has always been very satisfying, and while I cannot commit myself to anyone at this point, mainly because of my financial situation, nevertheless I feel that for the moment I am satisfied in this area.
(My personal score is: 20)
*Total Score 70*

If I sum up my situation: I am unemployed, I don't like it. At the moment I am still not desperate for money but will be if this goes on long enough. I have close friends and, while I failed in my marriage, I have some relationships which, on a superficial level, are satisfying for the moment anyway. I need some advice as to what I could do, if I don't get a job in the near future.

With the assessment of these five areas our self-understanding begins. Now, in Chapter 4, I shall outline some exercises in understanding, experiencing and observing ourselves in order to clarify further issues.

# 4 Exercises in Understanding, Experiencing and Observing Oneself

The following paragraphs, which I wrote ten years ago, seem to have as much relevance today as they did then:

> Man has many more resources within his past experience than he is using at any given time. This assumption is, of course, more applicable to people who feel at the point when seeking outside help that they have no resources left at all. Paralysis of human functioning is the result of a series of unsuccessful attempts to cope with the experiences of living; it follows that most people who feel themselves to be failures are conditioned to perceive themselves as such. No human life, however, in its continuum, consists of frustration alone. Lack of present self-effectiveness, however, may focus both intellectual and emotional attention on the negative aspects of living, and may create a delusion of global failure.
>
> When past knowledge is not available to a person, the (negative) powers of the unconscious may turn against him; but when the past becomes accessible, the unconscious becomes more of an ally and less of an enemy.*

There are periods in everybody's life, particularly in times of great changes like unemployment, redundancy and stagnation, when we feel at odds with ourselves and the world around. We may experience anxiety or fear and want to understand what this really adds up to, in addition to what has been outlined in Chapter 3. I find it very useful either to write down and state

* Eugene Heimler, *Survival in Society* (Weidenfeld and Nicolson, London 1975; Heimler Foundation and Cardwell Human Resources, 1983)

feelings as they come, or to dictate them into a tape recorder. In both instances, the most important part is when we either *read back* what we have written or *listen back* to the tape recorder, because, with either of these processes, further thoughts and ideas will come to mind which will help not only to clarify the situation but, more often than not, give some relief from some of the turmoil we experience.

I asked a man in North America to let me have such notes after I had explained to him how this process works. After the example I shall discuss the principles and the techniques involved.

## 1   Stagnation

*Step 1    State the problem as it feels to you.*
A man aged 50 writes:

> I don't understand what is happening to me. I am full of tension. I am afraid of going down the drain. I feel very helpless. I feel like crying but I can't. Inside me something cries as well as shouts. I sense some collapse and some disintegration. It is interesting that now that I have written these things down, things that I am really afraid of, there is some relief; perhaps I am not that helpless. Yesterday at the office I felt good for a while when I proved to myself that I was not that helpless. The inner and outer worlds are in turmoil. I show calmness to the outer world, but inside hurricanes move in me. There are times when I feel I may lose control. This feeling of tension and agitation came over me last week when a senior colleague told me that I had no chance of promotion in the near future. If I don't get it now I may never get it. Then I immediately felt the feeling of helplessness. I felt like hitting out, but was afraid to do so. I feel that I am just getting old without having achieved what I want. I really don't know what the future can bring. As I want to write down everything that comes to mind, what does come to mind is that I feel like a

baby. My fantasy is that I am in a baby state and I really see a picture – whether it's me or not I don't know – and I have terrifying feelings. How am I going to come out of this state and how can I stay in my job with my disappointment?

As I write these things down some sensual feelings or even sexual feelings occur. For some reason I have gone back into my baby state. But, for heaven's sake, I am not a baby; I can walk on my own legs. Now, for a minute I had the fear that I may not be able to walk. There is at times almost a phobia that I shall not be able to walk. But at the age of 50 I have to stand on my own feet and I am afraid.

I turn to God but I don't get release. I am seeking security, but at the moment I find none. I feel that my most dreaded feelings have been realised. I was vicious and was punished by being abandoned. That is how I feel. I am clashing with the fantasies of the past. I feel some relief now. I want to ask all the time, what can I do? But this is the only thing I can do, to write things down. When I was told that I was not really wanted I felt like a small child. It is good to be able to write things down; small children cannot do that. But how can I move myself away from that baby feeling? Is it possible at the age of 50 to be pushed right back to one's beginnings because of a sudden disappointment? Yes, it is possible, apparently. I go further – it is more than likely. But how is all this going to help me to be free of tension and fear? I don't know, but the very ability to spell this out is a help. It seems to me that the child in me needs to be pacified. How can I pacify myself? I don't know. Heimler says that one ought to read the stuff back or listen to it from a tape recorder. OK, I am going to see what I can do and what it will lead to. If I don't help myself no one can and then I am lost and I, an adult, don't want to get lost. This I am sure of. And this is, I suppose, one of my few remaining strengths.

*Step 2    Read through what you have written down (or listen back on the tape recorder) and whatever comes – feelings and thoughts – write them down on a separate sheet of paper.*

'. . . I don't understand what is happening to me . . .'

Of course I do. In the Government Service where I work I have managed to reach quite a high position, but there was this last final step which I hoped to achieve, and apparently I failed. I was quite taken aback by this and was angry and did not show it. I also seem to have problems with my third child; he is now 16 and is going through some kind of crisis – can't concentrate and generally feels very confused. This, too, upsets me, as I don't understand what is happening to him. I sense tragedy and collapse and disintegration too. So one thing and another hooked on to each other makes me feel very tense. I sense great relief now that I have been able to put these things down.

'. . . perhaps I am not that helpless . . .'

I have the irritating habit or pattern of losing the focus of my adult being when things crowd over me. So if I can really understand what is bothering me, I can take action. I can, for example, talk to Dr X about Max (my son), and I will also go to my Chief and find out what went wrong, so that next time I will have more knowledge about the situation; but in both instances I have to act and face the truth, face reality too. For some reason, initially, I had great difficulty in doing that.

'. . . fantasy in the baby state . . .'

I really see a small child in a cot. I fancy, somehow, that I am that child. Can one remember that far back? It doesn't matter really; but I do feel a kind of unity with that child. However, while I was writing, just for a moment, I felt total unity with that child; as I am looking from here aged 50, as I am writing this now, a distance appears between now and then. The fact that I recognise this distance also gives me a feeling of relief, so I am that child but that child is removed from me across time. And, although I am afraid I can't walk, that is absolute nonsense because I can. And I simply must not talk myself into something which is totally crazy. Yes, I have to stand on my feet and that means I have to face, and not run away from, my problems.

'. . . I turn to God but I don't get release . . .'

Now that is not true; I do. And it is not true either that I don't find any security, for the security is in me; after all I am not helpless. And it is also extremely childish of me to think that just because I was not wanted in my job I should feel like a small abandoned child. It is interesting to notice that the spelling out of these thoughts and feelings is helping me to gain control over myself and feel more of a whole.

'. . . how can I reach the child and pacify him? . . .'

Well, I am doing just that now, so I appear to have gone through two processes: one when I was totally inside the situation, and now as an observer. I am outside that situation, and being outside means to be an adult.

'. . . if I don't help myself I am lost and I don't want to get lost . . .'

Well, ten minutes ago I didn't know how to help myself, and now I do. I know exactly what steps I have to take, and I will take them. I really feel much better now.

In the above example a man looks at his life, at some of the turmoil, and seeks to find out why he feels helpless. He goes through two processes: in the first he puts down his problems on paper, so that in some ways he externalises some of the internal chaos experienced by himself; and in the second he looks at his externalised material and freely associates it with a number of thoughts, feelings and fantasies. I think it is relevant to note that although the person who *states* the problems and the person who *looks at* these problems is the same person, there is a difference between the experiencing self and the observing self.

## The Experiencing Self

Without recorded statement, much of our experience moves straight through us, without being digested. Invariably a great many experiences fall into the depths of our unconscious without this process of 'digestion'. Yet there are times when we are so overwhelmed by what appear to be unknown feelings and strange thoughts that we need to stop events and express them. We often attempt such expression by trying to think things out, but the trouble here is that too many varied thoughts and feelings may reach our consciousness at once, so that it becomes difficult to keep them in any kind of order. Writing things down, however varied the material may be, helps in some way with the selection and organisation of our internal material, and it also allows us to look back over this material later.

It seems that the purpose of consciousness is to create some logical order out of chaos. Consciousness needs solid structure, and writing offers such a structure. The same applies if, instead of writing, we speak our feelings and ideas into a tape recorder. To be able to formulate what appear to be puzzling, menacing and confusing ideas, on paper, is in itself a considerable relief. But the real benefit comes from a structured and disciplined examination of the statement.

## The Observing Self

Seldom are we able to observe ourselves in action. We are so busy experiencing life, and so many things are happening to us continuously, that we cannot observe what they are and we cannot make sense of them. Our society demands a continuous performance from us, and this performance, without occasional introspection, creates restlessness, because the meaning of life often escapes us. Eastern philosophies turn inwards, ignore the outer world and are concerned with inner events. This to my mind is equally frustrating (and almost impossible) for Western man. I feel that there should be a balance between experiencing and observing. The observing self can make use of experiences accumulated in the past. The observer observes with millions of experiences; thus the process is very creative. But if we can deepen our observations by allowing further free associations to occur, then a truly emotionally digested process results, which can be, and often is, very helpful indeed.

I advise people I teach to do this combination of statement and self-observation occasionally, in order to understand themselves better.

The combination of experiencing and observing has a further benefit, that is, the better understanding of others. This understanding is not only required in therapeutic work or, as stated in Chapter 2, in social situations, but is also important in work, unemployment, middle age human relationships and sexuality, so I need to speak about these before I return to the specific problems of unemployment and redundancy. Once you have understood the basic structure of how to proceed, and can feed back information about yourself to yourself, you can start to crystallise your problems. You should now be learning to recognise your own particular pattern of responses and be able to see some of the fields in which your own personal frustrations and satisfactions lie. Your own difficulties and solutions will always be unique to you.

## 2   Work Problems

Work is particularly important, for most of us spend more than half our waking lives at work. It looms large in our lives; it has enormous emotional significance for us all, and through it we can express deep-seated feelings. Some of us manage to do work we like, so that it does not feel like 'work' at all, but instead it becomes a pleasure, a satisfaction and an absorbing interest.

Most of us, however, struggle along doing the same job day after day. We are so deeply entrenched in the daily groove that we seldom stand back, look at why we are doing it, or consider changing. Then, perhaps, one day we feel utterly fed up with it all. We feel we are accomplishing nothing; that work is soul-destroying, self-destroying, and totally frustrating. All we want to do is give it all up and clear off. Sometimes a colleague's comments trigger off our gloom, or, as in the example given, we have been supplanted or passed over for promotion. Maybe we feel unwanted, neglected, or unable to satisfy the exacting demands of a boss. More often than not these feelings of futility build up slowly over a time, until they become more than we can bear.

Then we must assess whether work is really our only problem, or whether it stems from some other area of our lives. Then, if we come to the conclusion that it is work which is the basic difficulty, we must consider the possibilities. Can we change our place of work? Or change the type of work? Is it the job, the people, our attitudes or our aims which are off course?

Take a piece of paper and write down briefly what you have done and *achieved* since childhood. What were your original hopes, aspirations and dreams? Is there a pattern? Have you achieved anything which you set out to do? Are you even travelling in the right direction? Did you start in the right direction and then get side-tracked? Are you now in a job which could lead towards any of your hopes?

If there is no pattern, write down what your goals are today, at this moment, and how you feel they could be achieved. Whilst doing this, you must accept that new goals and new work mean a challenge and you must be willing to take up this challenge. Change may take time, it may not be easy, but you do not *have* to stay in an unsatisfactory job. With proper self-examination, planning and perseverance, a new goal can be achieved, and working towards this new goal may make the daily grind seem far more satisfying and interesting. It is never too late to start something new; but we must be prepared to pay the price, and it is this price which many people shy away from.

In assessing the importance of work in our lives, it is essential that we should understand how much of our deeper inner selves it expresses, or can express.

Through play a child learns about the world around him, and in his play he expresses his instinctive basic primitive feelings, his desire to learn, to explore, to succeed, to overcome frustrations which are common to us all. In his play the child acts out his desires for safety, for security, for achievement, his anger and aggression. He is working at two levels at once, the internal and the external, and all the while he is learning to build a bridge between these two levels. At the same time he is gaining new experiences and learning to cope with feelings of frustration and satisfaction; finding out how to turn negative feelings into positive ones. He is also acquiring a sense of purpose. But while the child sits in the nursery playing, he is being subjected to a wide variety of experiences from his parents, his brothers and sisters and all those around him; he is being thwarted or encouraged, bullied or loved. All these emotions, too, are being built into his personality.

Man's work is an extension of the child's play, and he brings to his work as a man all the emotions, drives, feelings and attitudes which have crystallised within him during childhood and adolescence. In his work he will express many of these feelings, not only in the work he chooses to do, but in the way he goes about his job. Some of these feelings will be conscious; others he will be unaware of. But in his work he is expressing his basic drives for power and importance, his skill, his knowledge, his curiosity and creativity. In his achievements and his struggles he is transforming negative frustrations into positive satisfactions wherever and whenever he can. He is seeking a meaning to life, a sense of purpose, and through his work he becomes part of the wider world around him.

Work, therefore, can be an outlet at three levels: for instinctive basic drives; for unconscious childhood echoes from the nursery; for present needs and desires. In work we express something of our yesterdays; through it we look for a chance to put old wrongs right and to transform past dreams into today's reality.

If we are thwarted in trying to express ourselves at work, if the work is totally unsuited to our aims and drives, if we have no opportunity to transform past dreams into present reality, then we may withdraw from life and become emotionally disturbed, or turn against society by anti-social behaviour. Then we may need some other form of expression away from work.

## 3   Middle Age and Work

But in our middle years we may discover another problem. Slowly the middle-aged begin to realise that there is no longer any need for a dialogue with the child within; that the interplay of past with present is over. Instead, new features have appeared and new dimensions opened up. People begin to question their motivations in work, and to feel that their achievements to date are of no real relevance or significance. They stand bewildered, not knowing which way to turn. The coping mechanisms which worked so well in the past no longer seem appropriate or effective. It is as if the batteries that kept the human machine going have run down and they do not know how, if at all, they can be recharged. It is a time of struggle and turmoil for many, as they search frantically for a new meaning to their lives, new aims and goals, or a last desperate chance to achieve unfulfilled ambitions. Those who come through this time of change develop a maturer, deeper, richer, personality.

This time of self-doubt and loss of confidence heralds dangers as well as new opportunities, for there is the danger that the turmoil may get out of hand and that the new opportunities for change will not be taken. It is a period of life when many change their jobs or develop new interests, for a new pattern is struggling to emerge in middle age. Life is less of a ping pong game between the past and the present and more concerned with the here and now, with meaning, maturity, with living and dying.

If you have reached this stage in life and are uncertain what to do, then ask yourself some questions about your job and your attitude towards it. Ask yourself all the questions that I have mentioned earlier in this chapter, and also whether you fit the job, or the job you? Has it answered any of your life-long needs or ambitions? Is there any chance of being able to do what you have always longed to do? If so, what will the cost be? Examine possible alternatives. Too many people put up with second best because they are afraid of change, yet often changes are imposed on us in any case. It often happens nowadays that redundancy coincides with middle age, and lack of planning and action may produce severe depression. This can be avoided if we concentrate on the opportunities ahead rather than feel useless about opportunities lost. It is never too late to change.

The following example concerns a man of 62 years. For 40 years he had been with the same firm, in the same clerical job. For 40 years he dreamed about using his ability to draw and to paint. He did a little of both, after a heavy week's work, but he lacked energy and stimulus. He had a growing family that needed him, and all the responsibilities that this entailed. But now, at the age of 62, the children had gone and there was only himself and his wife. Now she too felt empty, as if her task were finished and there were nothing more to do. He came to see me in some confusion. He spoke about his dreams of wanting to be an artist and how it was now too late. He felt empty and spent. Three more years to retirement, then perhaps he could, at last, do what he wanted. But now in the autumn of life three years seemed like eternity. His pension was the key issue. He could get *some* pension now but much less.

He listened to himself as I 'fed back' to him his own story. As he listened, it became increasingly clear to him that either he was going to take the risk now, or never. A few weeks later he had made a plan. He would retire now, take the reduced pension, go to Europe, draw and paint, and his wife would try to arrange some exhibitions for him. Three years later, at the age of 65, he had succeeded. He had many successful exhibitions, became a sought-after artist and his only regret was that he had not taken the plunge sooner.

You cannot, however, take the plunge without preparation and a reasonable plan. The safeguard is to write down and assess all the possible pros and cons.

The creation of a *plan* is the key issue. In order to arrive at it you need to be able to express as clearly as possible the reasons that lie behind the plan. I suggest that you divide this task into two parts:

1  an evaluation of past aspirations, hopes and fantasies using methods found in previous chapters; and
2  a feasible plan as to *what* and *how* to carry this out.

Into this plan you must calculate the risk element, and also what alternatives are open if by some bad luck things do not work out. You must not gamble away everything; that is what I mean by a *feasible plan*.

Spell out, preferably on paper, all the pros and cons and all the details of steps to be taken. When all this has been done, lock away the papers for a while and then discuss it with others – wife, family, friends – before any decision is taken.

In previous chapters I have spoken about the spurring of emotive forces behind our adult endeavours: how earlier experiences feed the flames for adult achievement. There comes, however, a time when some of the goals that we set out to achieve have been achieved and there is no more driving force for similar further achievement left in us. Some may have achieved their aims only partially, or not at all, and now they find that perhaps their unfulfilled ambitions were not that important after all.

This period of changing evaluation of past, present and future can be extremely painful, and critical for further growth and development. Whatever the answer that emerges for each of us, it will determine both style of life and internal harmony for many years to come.

The merging final part of our lives is concerned with *purpose* and *meaning*, appreciation of beauty and harmony, that we have a place where we fit into the order of things. This search for inner meaning and purpose, however, is not without pain. The nature of this pain will vary from individual to individual, and the ultimate resolution will also bear the mark of individuality. This inner change does not come about suddenly, and one cannot be sure exactly when it will begin; but both men and women in their fourth decade stand at the bottom of a hill, and it may take some time, months certainly, possibly years, before they arrive at the summit and see the land beyond. When we are in the middle of turmoil and change we can experience, and often do, a great deal of sadness and pain. For many decades so many of our actions were conditioned by instinctive, innate and childhood drives, and were influenced by parental and child-hood pressures, that many people find it difficult to say goodbye to such a long conditioned pattern of existence. Our earlier influences do not disappear completely, but their significance is of a different order of importance.

Women can identify definite physiological changes which take place heralding the end of the reproductive period, so they may find it easier to acknowledge some of the pain and conflict, anxieties and panics, than do men. Having gone through 'the change', they may begin to feel active and purposeful again, with different activities and with a different purpose. Many women nowadays start new careers at this particular stage of life, and the changing social climate gives them the opportunity to do so. Men, however, do not have *manifest* and dramatic biological changes. Nevertheless they seem to go through very similar processes, and as they cannot account for them in terms of physical changes, they are often more bewildered, more lost and more confused than women.

In the last few years I have been observing the lives of *many* middle-aged men. On the surface they do not behave markedly differently from, say, ten years ago. They go about their business as before, trying to be as busy; it is only on much closer enquiry that they will admit, even to themselves, the self-doubt and lack of purpose in their lives. They look back to their last ten years and wish that everything were the same, their energy enthusiasm, sexuality; and because it is not, they feel that something is going very wrong. Tradition, education (or the lack of it) and social conditioning have made men reluctant to talk about such personal problems. They are often afraid to admit to themselves that they feel beset by anxieties and panics. They do not understand why, when their competence is at its highest, they should feel doubt where no such doubt existed before. Often they present themselves to their doctors with vague physical ills; sometimes the energy that has hitherto been externalised into action actually hits people physically in more recognisable forms of illness which are often diagnosed as being psychosomatic, i.e., induced by emotions interacting with bodily functions. It seems that man has fallen into a trap which he has prepared for himself. Over many centuries men have built a philosophy about *what they should be like.* According to this, men are strong, women are weak; women were 'made' for sex, bearing children and looking after the family, men were 'made' to earn the family's living, succeed, and achieve. Women were supposed to be emotionally more variable, more unstable than men. This masculine megalomania harmed not only women but also the men themselves. Such a philosophy had to be built on complete denial of psychological bisexuality. *Thus men crippled themselves by denying their intimate and finer emotions.*

Now, in the middle years, these emotions break through, and at last claim their rightful place in the personality of men. Maturity is in a sense, the ability to accept and integrate what one truly is. Some men find such integration very difficult to achieve. So when they find that the work they are supposed to get satisfaction from does not give them the same sense of purpose, the same feeling as before, or that their livelihood is threatened; when they find that their physical powers are also on the wane, and when they experience 'instability' of feelings, and feel attacked by irrational forces from within which they can no longer keep at bay by continuous activities, then the questions 'Who am I?', 'What am I?', 'Where am I going?' or even 'Am I going anywhere at all?' become crucial.

It seems that this is man's last chance for personal integration, yet many people fight the ongoing changes sooner than admit them to themselves, making their lives critical, painful and confusing; and here, perhaps more than at any other time, *clarification* of what is going on is of great importance. If people do not learn to listen to others, to listen and to understand themselves, then it is unlikely that they will find a way out. Then there is the pathetic desire to remain young at all costs, or the temptation to move into a pit of depression. Such people do not find emotional fulfilment or spiritual awareness, however near it may be. It is perhaps at this stage more important than ever to use some of the 'methods' I have outlined in earlier chapters, in order to be able to evaluate the changing importance of work and the development of new interests and skills, to reach out towards the world with renewed finer feelings when the initial struggle for personal survival is almost over. It is more than important to prepare oneself slowly for retirement, because the sudden disappearance of defences like work, earning a living, fighting for survival, can throw man at the mercy of sudden internal powers which he may not be able to cope with. *You have to prepare for the autumn while summer's sun is still high in the sky.*

It is possible for you, through the various approaches that I have outlined, to crystallise your philosophy of life on the basis of your past experiences: to bring into being a solid platform which should give you a sense of security. I think it is very important to know where one stands. The crystallisation of this 'stand', through the various exercises that I have suggested, should give you a greater confidence that, after all, the meaning you once found in life is still there. You can then bring this new sense of meaning into your life, and this in turn will affect positively both your actions and your relationships with others. It seems that maturity in middle age means a development of a personal stand which is the accumulation of various experiences of living, so that you can see the world from your own personal viewpoint and not be overwhelmed by the view of others.

Michael, at the age of 54, had been in turmoil because he felt that in his job as a salesman he had not achieved what he could have achieved. He felt threatened by more aggressive, and not necessarily more able, young colleagues. At home with his wife and son he felt continuous tension, particularly when his son went out with friends, some of them young girls. At times he would look at his wife and notice how much she had changed during the last few years; yet, at the same time, he was surrounded by a world that spoke about enjoying the moment and not caring about tomorrow. Although his marriage was happy, he began to wonder in his great frustration whether he could not do still better and before going to sleep at night he would have fantasies about some superwoman who would answer all his needs.

When he began to evaluate his life, his success and his failure, he saw clearly that, although in the eyes of others he had not achieved all that much, yet he was appreciated by his family, who thought the world of him. He had managed to give his son an excellent education so that he could develop his gifts. He stood by his wife through thick and thin, and over the years he had done a lot and had had a strong feeling of duty and commitment.

As he listened back to his own voice he realised that the superwoman of his fantasy could not and did not exist in reality, and perhaps the superwoman was an echo of his earlier years when he longed for the mother whom he had lost when he was quite young. He was able to confirm his belief that to believe in right and wrong is humanly justified, and through observation of others during his five or so decades of living he could see that no one could ever find a perfect solution to a life situation. The greater strength that came from his self-observation was the feeling that all the coincidences in his life were extremely significant; that, without wanting to go into mysticism, he could see, or rather feel, that there was a clear pattern emerging: a pattern which was purposeful and helped to shape his destiny. He could also observe such a pattern in others.

Strengthened by his experiences regarding the acceptance of good and bad, he could state his problems more easily to his wife and she was very sympathetic and understanding. Having confirmed his sense of duty, achievement and failure, he felt the fascination of observing life itself, and decided to take notes in his free time on his observations. He did not particularly want to publish these but they furnished him with a strong interest in life. Michael, towards his mid fifties, found his platform, his stand.

## 4   Relationship Problems

Ted was 36 years old, recently unemployed, and his problem was now loneliness. In his own words: 'I am incapable of forming any kind of relationship either with men or women. I live alone, and the only living thing I have for company is my alsatian dog. I worked in a small town and lived some 20 miles away in a village. I was alone in a laboratory and hardly saw anyone all day, but at least I had people around me. At night I drove home, cooked my dinner and watched TV. Sometimes I talked to my dog. It was not living, I tell you, and since I lost my job, it's been worse.'

This pattern had been formed whilst quite young. At school he had always been 'the odd man out' because he had always declined to compete with his fellow students physically. He hated sport and all organised activity. Now he still hated everything that was 'organised'. Sometimes he would drive to his sister who lived 300 miles away; with her he could talk, but with no one else.

I asked him why he did not join some club or church activity. He answered: 'When I see two or more people together in a group I want to run. I'm afraid of crowds, I feel that they are going to swallow me up. People make me panic.'

Ted's problems, though perhaps extreme, are shared by many people. Many find it difficult to take the first step to overcome unreasoning panic induced by fear. When unemployment strikes an already vulnerable person, it is more important than ever that he should not be alone.

I asked Ted to imagine, however unpleasant it was for him, that he was at a large gathering, a party. At first he refused to 'play', but after a while he agreed.

TED:   I'm at this party. I'm standing by the door so if it becomes unbearable I can get out quickly. My head and my whole body feel strange . . .

ME:   Describe what it feels like to be standing there.

TED:   I can't.

ME:   Please try.

TED:   All those men and women talking to each other make me feel caged in. My throat is throbbing. My head aches.

ME:   What do you imagine these people think about you if they notice you standing there?

TED:   I don't wan't them to notice me because . . .

ME:   Because what?

TED:   I feel very angry.

ME:   You feel very angry with whom?

TED:   I hate them. I hate people. If I stayed long enough I shouldn't be responsible for what I might do . . . to them.

ME:   Do I understand you to say that you are not afraid of them, but rather of what you might do to them?

TED:   That's right.

We both kept quiet, and there was a very long silence. Then Ted spoke. He was back at school where the children teased him. They called him sissy and mummy's baby. When he got frightened and angry he would stammer slightly. He wanted to hide. I put it to him:

ME:   What you are saying is that as a child you had some nasty experiences with children; but are you a child now?

TED:    People never fully grow up; they only hide their nastiness better.

ME:     Do you feel grown up?

And there was silence again.

A few weeks later I asked him to imagine that he was at the same party and that he was searching for someone who was not too frightening. Uneasily he began to move inside the room in his imagination until he found another man about his age standing there, also alone. He wanted to go up to him and speak to him but didn't know what to say.

ME:     Tell him how you feel.

TED:    I can't.

ME:     Please try.

TED:    OK. I go up to him and say: 'We are both alone. Can I join you?'

ME:     How does he respond?

TED:    He seems quite happy. He felt at a loss like myself; but I don't know how to carry on with the conversation.

ME:     Simply tell him what's on your mind.

After a little while:

TED:    I'll tell him that I feel out of place at parties; does he feel the same way? He says he feels like that too.

So Ted made his first contact with others in his imagination.

He spoke a great deal about his hostile feelings and even remembered his pre-school days, and his dislike for his father and mother. Slowly he began to understand how he had built up a great mountain of aggression within himself which he had then displaced outside himself onto crowds and people. Eventually, after many long sessions, he succeeded in talking to people and so learnt to make relationships. He made some friends and found that he was not alone with his problems. Then he began to ask where he wanted to go with his life. He did not want to work in a laboratory ever again!

Often fear of others covers up some fear within ourselves. It is not unusual to feel anxiety amongst people. It is partly the way we are brought up in relation to others and partly the fear of our own hostility that prevents us from making relationships. Sometimes we become so afraid of our anger that we exaggerate its importance in our minds and think that something must be very wrong with us. The fear of anger is worse than the fear of meeting people. We need, however, to recognise and understand ourselves a little before we can move into positive action. Sometimes the nature of our work, as in the case of Ted, increases hostility and isolation. For him, losing his job represented a new opportunity, a new potential; but in his position we need someone we can confide in easily with little or no reservation, particularly when, due to unemployment, we have no mates or colleagues. Not to have someone to talk to can feel like being in solitary confinement. Ted's problem was his shyness: *his work an expression of his failure with relationships.*

Not only work problems and redundancy may cause anxiety and depression: it may be the other way round; and we need contact with people to clarify which way the problem really lies. That is why Ted came to see me in the first instance; and that is why, before helping him with his work problems, I needed to concentrate on his loneliness and isolation.

For many men and women who, because of their earlier problems and lack of choice, have been working in a field totally unsuited to them, redundancy may be the only potential to finding an alternative expression of their personality, either in new work, and/or in some satisfying life task. It is, however, very important for us all to see that our work problems are interwoven with other aspects of our lives. In Ted's case it was relationships, but it could have been family problems, health problems or sexuality. There is a continuous interplay between the five areas of life satisfactions and frustrations which I outlined in Chapter 3.

## 5 The Effect of Unemployment on Sexuality/Marriage and Family

Nineteen years ago, in 1966, I noted that there were victims of automation, modernisation and of industrial closures. This I considered to be one of the biggest problems of our time, a problem about which industry must take action or thousands of people will suffer unnecessary misery. In my work I saw an often-repeated pattern which started with rumours of a factory closing and ended in an individual's breakdown. I noticed that sudden unemployment affected a man's *sexual functioning*, as I have already mentioned.

The following is a typical example of such cases. Take a railwayman of about 35, a decent and industrious man, with no history of psychological illness, happily married with children, at the height of his working skill. He hears talk of redundancy and begins to show signs of anxiety. This anxiety state is new to him and affects his relationship with his wife. He begins to drink a bit more, becomes short-tempered and irritable and throws the blame on the powers that be. He knows change is inevitable but he cannot reconcile himself to it.

Then unemployment sets in and he is offered the prospect of re-training or of moving to another district. At this stage, the idea of uprooting or of re-training creates a reactive depression. This phase is tolerated by his wife, whose maternal feelings are aroused, but at a point when the man finds them hard to accept. He has no desire to yield to emotion. As the wife's sexual desire increases his depression causes his own to decrease. The result is marital friction. The man becomes impotent and because of this considers himself impotent at all levels – both in his private life and as regards work. He is ashamed of this situation, reluctant to talk about it, and if a job turns up six months later, he is incapable of accepting it. The only hope for rehabilitation in cases such as this is to try to concentrate on the marriage, making it clear that neither party is to blame, but both are victims of circumstances.

What implications does this type of situation have for industry, I asked in 1966. All over the country old industries are being run down and new ones are developing in their place. It is the employees from the old who have been through an unsettled period, who will be working in the new and for some time may have considerable emotional problems. But who will help thousands of people with all the problems which arise in their sexuality, marriage or family life? I was convinced that the threat of change and the continuum of change was the root cause of absenteeism. I saw that there was an urgent problem which needed to be tackled at national level for both human and economic reasons. To mitigate the effects of change, I suggested that, as soon as an industry knows it is going to close down, discussions should take place at all levels to decide on the best course of action for employees. Advance planning helps remove the damaging effect of uncertainty and enables early arrangements to be made for re-training. *I also suggested human relations training at all levels so that management realises the full consequences of change on the people involved.* (Today, in 1985, I think that trades unionists should also learn about human relations, along the lines discussed in this book.)

I also spoke in June 1966 about modern industry's claiming another set of victims: those who can no longer find any creative satisfaction in work. Into this category I put the aimless youth and hooligans of our age. I said that if nothing were done about them, if there were no concerned and trained people to help, I foresaw a very dangerous and violent society by the end of this century, when working hours would have been considerably reduced and people would have more leisure on their hands. To overcome this problem, workers must be given a clear picture of the part they play in production, however monotonous and repetitive their particular job may seem. Alternatively, they must be given some other outlet or interest outside work. The drifting youngsters of our society were failing to respond to admonitions to return to work; but provided they had an interest in *something*, they could usually be talked back to work through this interest. Remember: this was in 1966!

Now it is not uncommon, either in 1966 or in 1985, for a father to feel useless, the marriage to become shaky as a consequence, and sons and daughters to act out their own resultant feelings of desperation, so that what was once a home becomes a battle ground of bitter, confused emotions. Where is the potential in such a situation, where everything is bleak, destructive and hopeless?

There cannot be potential in the *general* situation that evolves, but only in *each* individual family member's seeking and eventually finding his or her significance and relevance. If, for example, I had the chance and the financial resources to train unemployed men and women in 'unemployment counselling' to become facilitators* to others, to help them to find their significance, then most of the pain and confusion of redundancy (like the railwayman I quoted) experienced as defeat might be turned into personal victory for the self and for others.

I now consider training in the methods outlined here to be very significant and relevant for unemployed people, so that care and guidance can come from those who are in the same boat as the 'guided'. There will never be enough professionals to do this work, nor are they best suited to carry it out. Professionals could act to these 'unemployment counsellors' as consultants or supervisors.

---

* 'Facilitator' is the name I give to the person listening to and 'mirroring back' what is being said by the person engaged in exploring and crystallising his own problems.

# 5  Fragmenta Vitae, *and Forming a Plan of Action*

## Significant Events

The way in which we interpret events depends a great deal on our emotional state. If we are in an enthusiastic and positive frame of mind, then what happens to us is likely to appear in a more positive light. If we are tense, anxious and afraid, then everything tends to be coloured grey and seem threatening and worrying. Inevitably some experiences are in their very nature likely to make us feel anxious. If we meet these experiences when we are already full of apprehension, the result may be disturbing and very distorted. It is important, therefore, to understand how we perceive certain experiences and to learn how they affect us so that we are prepared.

In this chapter I want to examine with you those events in your life which are likely to cause you unusual emotions, particularly in connection with 'job hunting', interviews for a job, or any other great upheaval in your working life, redundancy or stagnation. Instead, therefore, of expressing thoughts and feelings in generalised terms, *this is a method of concentrating on those events which have significant personal relevance to you.*

Events in the immediate past do not have the same significance when experienced, as they do *when we look back at them* at a later date. Certain events will be more loaded with significance than others, and the importance we give to them is highly personal and subjective. If, for instance, you and your spouse were to go away on holiday together and spend all your time doing the same things, you would still be likely to choose quite different episodes as being of particular importance to you. Even if you did hit on the same experiences, their subjective significance to each of you would be different.

What this method involves is the examination of some small experience in the recent past that was significant for you. It is important that it should have some particular significance, not be just any event, so it may be that you can do this exercise only occasionally, when confronted with overwhelming emotions.

From among the past few days, choose a short period in which something relevant happened to you. The shorter the time period, the more compact the experience will have been – somewhere between half an hour and an hour would be quite enough for our purpose.

Then write down everything which happened to you in that hour, say: your feelings, actions and thoughts. (If you have a tape recorder, then use that.) You will find that it is much easier to do this if you write in the present tense, as though you were living through this old experience in the here and now. This inter-action with time helps to activate details which might otherwise be forgotten. Having selected the event, move back into that time in your imagination and write down everything you *possibly* can.

Reviewing a past event like this will not only give you greater insight into yourself, but will also sensitise you to a fuller perception of all events, both in the past and in the future, for by recalling to mind a mass of details, you train your mind to think, to remember, to notice and to evaluate, and you will eventually find that you will also be more alert to future events when they take place.

When you have written down all the details, have a little break; stretch your legs, have a cup of tea or do something completely different. Then read through what you have written sentence by sentence. If something new occurs to you, record it on a separate sheet of paper. You may find that your second thoughts grow and grow until they exceed your first recollections. Then read through the whole mass of your observations – all the feelings, thoughts, ideas and comments which have been triggered off by recalling this past event – and try to formulate a meaning. What has it taught you about yourself? Are you surprised by the data which you find significant and relevant? Can you now see why you chose this particular event?

Here is an example. This comes from a 39 year-old married market researcher, George, who recalls a significant event from his near past: an episode with Brian, a senior colleague at work.

*Statement 1*

Events yesterday morning between 11 a.m. and 12 noon.

I'm sitting by my desk writing my report. I look out of the window from time to time and it is raining. I look at the figures in front of me, columns and columns of statistics, and I feel that I would rather be at home with Jill. I have a vision: I am ill, lying at home tucked in a warm bed, and she is sitting by my side and is reading to me. A kind of blissful peace. I think: 'Why the bloody hell couldn't I have a cold?' Then, still looking at the figures, I think: 'Why do I need to be ill to stay at home? After all, I could pretend that I was ill just for a day.'

At this juncture Brian (a senior colleague) comes in and says that Les (the boss) feels that we can't last out much longer. If the economic situation goes on for the next six months like this, we'll all have to pack up and look for other jobs. As I sit there trying to look at the figures, I feel alarmed. After all, I have been with this firm for five years now and, generally speaking, I like the work and I like the people around me. I remember suddenly that I'll be 40 in the spring and firms like to have younger people – will I get another job? All this is what I feel and think but what I actually say is: 'You were always a pessimist. In six months' time the situation could take a turn for the better.'

To this Brian says that all indications are that it will be worse, and I tell him that it's no good worrying about it now. But Brian is still worried.

There is a long silence now, and suddenly I feel guilty for

having wished a few minutes ago that I was at home. I don't know why I feel this but I do. I see the raindrops moving down the windowpane, forming little rivulets. I wish that Brian would go to hell, but he sits down in the chair in front of my desk, puts both hands on his neck clasped together, and just looks into nothingness, which really irritates me. I feel I ought to say something, but what? Now I would like to carry on working but I can't concentrate.

Brian asks me if I want a cup of tea. I say that I do, thank you very much. I now know that for the next 20 minutes I will have to spend my time with him and I don't want to, yet there is no escape.

He 'phones Jane and says: 'We are ready for it.' He means the cup of tea but the way he says 'we are ready for *it*', for reasons which I don't quite understand, makes me irritable. I would like him to go away or I would like to disappear but I can't.

I don't quite know yet why this episode is significant to me but it is. I am now going to look at what I have written and see what comes out.


## Statement 2

I will record only my thoughts and feelings in connection with what I have said. I don't particularly like my desk. It is not big enough; it's all cluttered and crowded. When I have some papers to work on I have to carry other papers to a chair. This annoys me. I think people should have the right conditions to work in.

I don't know why I find it so difficult to get into the work. And I don't understand why I feel so . . . how shall I say, lonely. Yes, sitting there in the grey-lit room I do feel lonely. I remember that when I was learning to read and write at school one morning, it was heavy and dark outside, and then the teacher put on the light and somehow it all became cosier. Things don't really centre around my work but around Jill. Since the children arrived we haven't been able to reach each other in the same way as before. I like the kids, but there is no doubt that they make heavy demands on us both. By the time we get to bed both of us are exhausted. I am really trying to figure out how I could help Jill and I haven't come up with anything yet. Is this how married couples must live at our age? We can hardly go out in the evenings because it is so difficult to find babysitters. And Jill is eleven years younger than I am. She, more than I, would like to get away from it all. The heart of the whole matter is that I would like to create the conditions for us to be able to spend more time together, and all I can come up with is to pretend that I am ill in order to be able to do so. I find this childish on the one hand, and quite pathetic on the other. This is not how we imagined it would be when we got married. The only time Jill is free is when the kids are in school, and then I'm at work. I keep looking at these rotten figures in front of me. I feel like getting up and walking out. If only just once in a blue moon we could be as we were, but no bloody luck.

Although it is true that Brian is a pessimist, I know he is right. The firm will fold up, perhaps even get rid of me before the six months is up, and then what? There is a big mortgage on the house, and we bought the carpets and the things in the kitchen on the never-never. Financially we would be in a very bad way. I should be able to do something about this, but what? I can't expect Jill to go out to work. We discussed the possibility of her doing some typing at home but then she would be even more tired and irritable.

My sexual interest in Jill has dropped. The atmosphere is just not right. When I'm at home my future preys on my mind; although I try consciously not to worry about the future, I do.

Although Brian is a decent sort, sometimes he irritates

me. He's right, but he speaks as if he were at a funeral all the time. Mind you, he is in an even worse situation than I am because he is much older than me, and apart from his wife and children he also has to support his elderly mother.

I want the tea but I don't want to drink it with Brian. The way he ordered it irritates me.

Now what does it all add up to? That I am in a bit of a mess, personally as well as job-wise. I mustn't wait until the axe falls but do something now. I have got to make a move. Somehow I must also arrange with Jill that occasionally we spend a few hours alone together. It would be nice to have a job where I could work in the afternoons and evenings and be free in the mornings, but what kind of jobs are available? So the issue is clear: I must make a move and try at the same time to sort things out at home.

Now let us try to see what George's 'significant event' is about.

1    There is a sense of restless longing for his wife.

2    Irritation with a 'pessimistic' colleague, who in fact may be quite realistic.

3    *Recognition* of this reality and the worrying questions about the future.

4    He says at the end: 'So the issue is clear. I must make a move, and try at the same time to sort things out at home.'

What George had in fact done, a few days after the episode with Brian, was set down on paper this event which he felt was significant to him. The relevance of the episode *was not*, however, what it seemed on superficial retrospection (his irritation with Brian), but was that *his irritation and restlessness covered up a denied anxiety about an insecure future.* If George had just vaguely remembered the events of that afternoon, what he would have probably recalled was 'bloody Brian ordering the tea'. ('The way he ordered it irritates me. I don't know why.') Recalling the totally irrelevant and misleading (displaced) feelings about the tea would not have allowed him to get to his real concern.

The episode or event, fully understood, prepared George, by alerting him to face reality and to be *ready* to take steps. It is so often that we are trapped by our own short-sighted ignorance.

## Fragmenta Vitae (Slices of Life)

The 'Fragmentum Vitae' or 'Slice of Life' is an extension of the 'Significant Event'. While the 'Significant Event' brings us to the *core* of our problems, the FV (Fragmentum Vitae) can give us hints, or more, about the resolution of our problems. In my work I often use the FV with my clients to connect past dreams with present realities, irrespective of whether the problems presented centre around unemployment, redundancy or stagnation. The FV which is done in professional work is often more elaborate than what I present to you here, just as the professional use of my full Scale is more elaborate than what I introduced about the idea of the Scale in these pages. Nevertheless, even in the simplified version which I am putting to you now, it can be quite effective in sorting out what kind of work or life task we would be suited to follow.

The FV consists of the following interconnected phases:

1  *A statement* by you covering, say, a half-hour 'slice' of your last twenty-four hours. (Naturally the recording need not be that long.)
2  Recording the selected material either by writing it down or by using a tape recorder.
3  After this recording, reading through what has been stated (or listening back to the tape).
4  Summarising reactions to the recorded material.
5  When a *theme* presents itself, bearing this theme in mind and recalling an event from *earliest childhood*, then recording this, as in point 2.
6  As in point 3.
7  Seeing if any connection exists between the theme (point 5) and this early experience, and recording this, too.

8   Seeking a *positive* and *constructive* summary aiming at a plan
to resolve our difficulties. Pessimism and any other negative
attitude here should be avoided. No solution in our work or
other situation can come about as a result of pessimism.

As an example of how the FV is done, let us see how George,
having recorded his 'significant event', set about trying to plan
solutions to his predicament. This FV was done about two
weeks after his initial recording.

1   *A statement covering a half-hour 'slice' of your last twenty-four hours*

GEORGE:   When I came home last night about 7 pm, Jill
was rather short tempered and quite depressed. She said that since the morning she
had not had a minute to sit down, that she
was just running around in circles, she did
one thing and then another and yet again
another, and she did not know in the end
what she had been doing exactly, and with
what results; in any case, what is it all about?
I asked her what she meant, 'what is it all
about', and she answered that her life is an
unending chore without any release whatsoever and that she is fed up. I went to my room
and lay down and tried to calm myself. I, too,
had had a difficult day. It is now very clear
that the firm will close down and that very
soon I shall be without a job. Like Jill, I go
through my own days with a bitter taste in
my mouth. I feel that I am wasting my time
and I ought to be looking for something else,
but I really don't know what to look for and
what this something else could be. Colleagues whom I have known for years are
unemployed and, though some are even
younger than me, cannot get a job. There is

the question of whether I can ever find another job in my own field and this raises a question which fills me with a great amount of anxiety: what else can I do? I am trained for this, and I am not at all sure what else I could actually do. I would have liked to discuss it with Jill last night, but obviously I could not. So I stayed in my room contemplating these things. One thought followed the other and I just could not get anywhere. I thought it would be a good moment to try to do a 'Fragmentum Vitae'.

I went down and asked Jill at about what time we would be eating, and she said that dinner would not be ready until about eight. I asked if she wanted me to help with anything, and she then said that she had put the children to bed and perhaps I would just like to see whether they were all right, and there was nothing more that she wanted me to do. I asked her also whether she would be free to talk later on, at which she burst into tears, and then I tried to console her. I took her into my arms and we stood there in the kitchen for a few minutes while she sobbed bitterly. Then she turned to me and said that she was sorry to give me such a rough time when she knew that I, too, must be going through hell. I confirmed this and said that was the reason why I wanted to talk to her. I felt quieter because she, too, seemed to have quietened down quite a bit after her crying.

I went up to see the children. They were upset at having been sent up so early, but they played happily with me for a while, and then I kissed them goodnight and went back to my room and decided to make a plan; and when I came down I found Jill in a much better mood. I shared with her the uncertainty and insecurity that I am experiencing. We talked for quite a while, and then we both felt very very exhausted and went to sleep without really resolving anything.

I shall now try to use this period of yesterday as my statement (first step to the Fragmentum Vitae). I must register here that I do this with a great deal of ambivalence, because I have doubts whether any kind of exploration of this kind could really resolve anything. But as I cannot think systematically about my problems, I need some kind of structure and some kind of discipline, so irrespective of how I may feel, I will carry on and see what all this may mean.

2   *Recording the selected material either by writing it down or by using a tape recorder.*

GEORGE:   I have done that just now.

3   *After recording, reading through what has been stated or listening back to the tape.*

GEORGE:   I have just read through what I have written down and I have various feelings which I will now summarise under category 4.

4   *Summarising reactions to the recorded material.*

GEORGE:   What I see clearly is that both Jill and I are in a crisis. It is very likely that Jill, knowing what our situation is, is worried about it, just as I am, and cannot see how she can help. And she feels that she is stuck and 'running round in circles'. She is desperate, very upset, and it makes me feel very, very inadequate. If I cannot get myself out of this mood, I may become very depressed. So it is important for me to be able to see and observe that there is basically nothing wrong between the two of us, but that the present critical situation is upsetting us all in our respective ways. We can share and we can speak about things even though we cannot yet find a solution. This is very encouraging and gives me a feeling of strength. The way we were talking to each other last night in bed gave me a very deep feeling of love and connectedness with her, but, at the same time, it crossed my mind that God alone knows whether we shall be in the same house, or even in the same bed, in, say, a year's time, and that again made me feel very tense and anxious.

5   *When a theme presents itself, bearing this theme in mind and recalling an event from earliest childhood. Then recording this as in point 2.*

GEORGE:   The theme that presents itself is really very simple. I am going to lose my job, and I need seriously to consider alternatives while there is still time. As Jill feels so very unhappy in her own right, being at home and feeling useless, one theme that emerges from it all is, how could Jill and I, together, somehow form a partnership and work together from home. (As I write this down I feel that this is very, very unrealistic and not even possible.) Now, the first image that comes to my mind from my childhood: I may be four or five years old, I am not sure, but I see myself as a pretty small fellow. It is a rainy afternoon and the girl next door, who can't be more than four, has brought over her 'shop'. This is a tiny little replica of a shop; various little drawers contain various little items. There she is, there I am and also another little boy whose name I forget. Anyway, there are the three of us playing 'shop'. I am pulling the drawers out and pouring the contents on the floor. Our girl friend is very upset about this and says that everything should remain in the little drawers. I can't understand this. What is the point of playing shop if we cannot see what is in the drawers? I get annoyed about this, and so does the other boy. Yet the girl insists that if we play shop, we can only open the drawers when one of us boys buys something. She says that we have got to make some paper money and she is cutting up pieces of coloured paper and making it out to be money. I find this very silly because in one of her drawers she has some 'play' money and I would like to use that. She says that this is not fair because this money is hers, and that we have to use the paper money. This disagreement goes on for a while until I say to her, 'I don't want to play this any more, I want to have my own shop.' This is all I can recall. (It is interesting to note that I had not thought of or remembered this episode before.)

6　*After recording, reading through what has been stated.*

GEORGE:　I read through what I have written down here about my memory and I remember very clearly now the feelings I had: the annoyance, the anger about every step of our 'game': the little girl's insistence that no drawers should

be opened, that we should not use her money
but should use some silly paper as money. All
this, as I am writing, creates in me a feeling of
frustration, anger and disappointment.

*7   Seeing if any connection exists between the theme in point 5 and this
early experience, and recording this, too.*

GEORGE:   Well, there is a theme, a very, very important
theme indeed. At first it appears to me as
nonsense. Wouldn't it be possible for Jill and
me, in fact, to buy some kind of a shop where
she could help? We could sell this house –
although we have a mortgage, we would have
enough to make a down payment on a
tobacco or confectionery shop, a newsagent
or a combination of all these, and then we
could have a flat, perhaps above the shop.
Then arrangements could be made that we
would look after the shop and work there
alternately. Interestingly, this idea of having
a shop had not occurred to me. As I write it
down it still sounds an impossible proposi-
tion, and yet it may very well be feasible. If
we had a shop it would still, in the long run,
give me the opportunity to undertake some
kind of part time work, but the shop would be
our 'bread and butter'. Now the question is
whether Jill would find this idea feasible. The
longer I think about it, the more I see that
this is not only feasible but, perhaps, under
the present circumstances, the only thing
that we could do.

*8   Seeking a positive and constructive summary, aiming at a plan to
resolve the difficulties. Pessimism and any other negative attitude here
should be avoided.*

GEORGE:    Well, my summary is this: I don't really know
whether I have been thinking of this shop in
some kind of unconscious way and that is
why I have produced this particular memory,
or if the memory came up and produced in
me the feelings that I had when I was a child,
of wanting to 'play shop' on my own. But
whichever is the chicken or the egg, the fact of
the matter is that *here is something to be considered very seriously*, and it is very important
that all the pros and cons, details, financial
possibilities, and also details in relation to
Jill's function in the shop and my own, ought
to be carefully looked at and worked out point
by point.

This is not exactly the ultimate ideal that I
would have chosen, but there is some attrac-
tion in being my own master and having my
own 'drawers' filled with things which I can
open up and sell. This is something I need to
discuss with Jill very seriously.

What happened subsequently, months later, was that Jill,
after very careful thought and long discussion, decided that this
idea might just work. In the beginning she was not too enthusiastic about it, but the more and longer they thought about it,
the better she liked it, and she could see a balanced division of
being together with George and also being able to attend to the
household while George held the fort – enabling him, perhaps,
to do some kind of occasional or part time job.

This example about the shop is just one of many ideas which
may come up during the FV. However, it may be that several
kinds of FVs are needed before a clearer image and picture from
the past appears which can give a message to the present. You
should not go into the FV thinking that you will immediately

receive answers to very important questions. Just allow the points to be stated and then eventually see whether or not *the past, your own childhood, may give a guidance to your career in the present and for the future.*

While some people are able and capable of achieving this by themselves, others may not be able to use their imagination in a disciplined way without outside help. The 'Fragmentum Vitae', however, would clarify certain feelings from the past which might be useful for the realities of the present, even if the results are not going to be as dramatic as George's shop.

Whether the FV gives quick, immediate or delayed answers to some of the problems of unemployment, redundancy and stagnation, it is my experience that doing this, together with all the other approaches I have outlined in this book, can be very helpful in clarifying where we are, where we were and where we are going. I myself can be very thankful for having stumbled on the 'Fragmentum Vitae'. Twenty years ago I was working at the Health Department of Middlesex County Council when, within a few months, both London and Middlesex County Councils were to fold up and thirty-three new London Boroughs emerge in their place. I was in this job for many years and progressed from being a Psychiatric Social Worker to Psychiatric Social Work Organiser. The new emerging situation threatened my livelihood as well as my future aspirations. I did not know for some time what I should do. It was on the cards that I would be transferred to one of the London Boroughs, but whether this would give me the opportunity of furthering my work as I had done in Middlesex was a big question mark.

Like George, I needed to connect my past aspirations with the present, so that I could perhaps work out for myself a more satisfying future. At that time, in 1964, I had the chance to settle in California. I had, however, serious reservations about leaving England, both for emotional and practical reasons. Emotionally I felt that I had already uprooted myself once when I came from Hungary to Britain, and to do it for a second time would have been too much. Secondly, because I knew quite a lot about the United States, as I had spent a great deal of time there, I had doubts about how steady my job would be; furthermore, I did not want to expose my son to the possibility of fighting in Vietnam.

So I turned to the FV to see whether I would come up with some suggestions as to which way I should go. As I was recording most of the problems which I mentioned here, the childhood association that came to me was the following: I was a little boy, under five, running in a field, a beautiful field in high summer, trying to catch butterflies. As I looked back on that episode – the sun-soaked field with its flowers and myself trying to catch butterflies – I sensed an extraordinary freedom. Now, in connection with my dilemma of going to the United States or staying in England, this feeling of freedom that came from the past gave me the final solution and determined what the rest of my life should be.

I decided that I would neither stay in England for good nor go to the United States for good; but in order to preserve my freedom, I would try to find a solution in which I would spend roughly equal amounts of time in each continent. I did not know then whether this was at all possible. It was an unusual solution by any standard, but I had it clearly in my mind and, with that clarity of thought and feeling, in a relatively short space of time I had found a solution: to spend half the year in Britain and half the year in Canada and America. Without this feeling of childhood freedom in the field, I could not have brought my mind to the kind of freedom that I needed and wanted. It gave me the stimulus *to sensitise me to opportunity*. It made me aware that I might suggest to various prospective employers what my ideas were, and not wait for a job to 'turn up' which would fit my ideas and dreams. I had to create the idea of a job in my mind first. I have never regretted what I have done. It gave me the freedom I sought: freedom that I had only found a long time ago in that field on that summer's day.

Had I waited for an advertised job or jobs to fit my need for freedom, I now know that it would never have come. Such jobs are simply not available. But with that 'Fragmentum Vitae' in mind, in the course of time I have created for myself 'the job of jobs'. In consequence, *in 'Fragmenta Vitae', the emerging past may not give a direct answer as in the case of George and the shop; it may be a stimulus to fulfil an ambition which has lain dormant in the depths of the past.*

Do not be disappointed if the answers do not come at once. And do not expect that there will always be answers. But the connection between the past and the present potentially contains 'messages' which can define and determine the future course of events in your life. The 'Fragmentum Vitae' should *only* be used for the exploration of your problems in connection with unemployment, redundancy and stagnation. In other words: use it for down-to-earth, practical solutions – do not attempt to sort out marriage or other emotional problems; that way can get you into a muddle.

# 6   *Potential for the Young*

## 1   Utilisation of the 'Negative'

In previous chapters I have discussed the importance of understanding our human needs: of respecting them, of evaluating in
a more systematic fashion the satisfactions, both great and
small, that we may have, in order to improve the quality of our
lives. I have spoken about active listening as a prelude to our
understanding of ourselves, and also about the importance of
distancing ourselves from our problems. I have tried to show
you how everything in our experience is connected with everything else, but how we can be hypnotised by one particular area
as being overwhelmingly pressing, to the exclusion of some or
all of the others. In this connection I have briefly presented
some thoughts about unemployment, human interaction,
middle age and sexuality. In Chapter 5, on the 'Fragmenta
Vitae', I outlined how we can make sense of past and present
experiences by connecting them. If, in our youth, we had received imaginative preparation at the right time and at the right
place – i.e., in school – could not the teachers have unearthed
the hidden potential in us *before* we find ourselves, as adults,
in a cul de sac?

I am sure that adequate preparation for adult existence
would have helped a great deal to reduce the confusion we feel
in facing the many changes which confront us today. Though
many of these changes could not be easily predicted say forty
years ago, nevertheless, neither past nor present generations
were taught how to identify and respect the *hidden gift* which
most of us carry within us.

What happened in our past education cannot now be altered,

but perhaps this is the chance to offer a different, more dynamic education to those children and young adults who are in our schools today and tomorrow, and to those who are planning to enter various training schemes in the future. What is this 'different and more dynamic education'?

So far I have referred in the previous pages to frustration being the spur to creativity. I would like to explain this further.

Very early experiences, though forgotten, are still with us today. Some of these were perceived as positive, others as negative. In time, the repeated *patterns* of good and bad experiences crystallised and began to shape our early attitudes, feelings and character. The possible permutations in the outcome are endless; each is always unique, and bears the mark of individuality. In consequence, differing reactions to parental influence, even in the same family, develop into dissimilar patterns in the various members of the family. It is seldom that parents and children, for example, would in retrospect view significant events in the same way. Subjective perception of reality varies between family members.

If a child, for example, develops very early in his/her life a pattern of anger against the parents and environment, (naturally this does not mean that he or she did not experience positive feelings as well,) this anger, manifest or hidden, will be his or her companion into adult life. It may cause problems of various degrees, or it may simply 'sit' there waiting to burst out. If this anger does not find a creative and socially useful expression in reality, it remains a hidden gift: *a hidden potential*; or else it may burst out into destructive and anti-social behaviour, with catastrophic consequences.

Yet the anger and aggression are a potential gift *if they are recognised* as being capable of some unique and creative expression. What is needed is that the teacher should recognise *the gift behind the mask* of, say, very passive or, on the other hand, very aggressive, behaviour.

When such recognition has occurred, the teacher can help the child or young man or woman to find the structure, the framework in which the child may *use his anger with imagination and self control.*

Psycho-analysis and other psycho-dynamic approaches use an extended relationship between analyst and client, with the aim that through the process known as 'transference', early unconscious problems may be resolved in the client. This was, and still is, one of the most creative and effective approaches of our age; but the time and finances involved are considerable, and would not be available to the millions of unemployed, young and not so young. They operate on a different principle from what I am presenting here. To oversimplify it: they aim to *resolve* the problem, aggression, while I have found that we can *use* our problems (frustrations) as a spur to do something else, and so resolve them by some activity or action which is satisfying. In doing so, the increased satisfaction *in the here and now* has an important and very interesting effect on our perceptions of the past. It alters the negative perceptions of the past, so that memories and impressions of 'yesterday' may be replaced by positive perceptions today. I put 'yesterday' between inverted commas because I have found that our 'yesterdays' are in fact always with us in our todays. Using the concept of *time* for the separation of experience can be confusing, since *all* experience is in the present, conscious or unconscious. What we call memories may appear to have occurred at various stages of our lives, but the *feelings* created by these memories are with us all the 'time'. This 'time interaction' can be clearly seen by those who use my 'Scale of Social Functioning'. There are five general questions on the Scale relating to childhood experience:-

1   When you look back, do you feel happy about your child-hood?
2   Did you have a secure childhood?
3   Did you feel that there were people in your childhood who really cared?
4   On the whole, do you think your childhood was a good preparation for adult life?

5   Would you want your family to turn to you with their problems?
(The answers can be 'yes', 'perhaps' or 'no', and scored 4, 2 and 0 respectively.)

One would think that as these questions are related to *past experience*, they are unalterable in terms of response at any time. Yet changes do in fact occur in the 'unalterable past' according to the satisfaction/frustration perception of the *present*. In short: *our perception of the past changes according to our perception of the present, and our perception of the present depends a great deal on whether or not we can use ourselves creatively in our environment and in society in general.* As I said before, it is not only in our positive that our potentials lie; in fact often there is *more* potential lying dormant in our negative. The question is, does society offer our potentials creative, satisfying outlets?

The approach I am presenting here is not necessarily within the professional therapist's domain; in fact perhaps the most important aspect of it is that it would concern the teacher and the educational system first and foremost, and even the ordinary 'layman'. In my book *Mental Illness and Social Work*, in the 1969 edition, I say as follows:

> We can, however, now see from the work we have done that, provided we are able to release frustrations into creativity – not necessarily in the artistic sense – we can bring about a new attitude to life. This may mean for the unemployed man that work is not going to be the means of expression of his creative needs, but he may, with the help of the educational system and other experts, be enabled to find a new *life task* which will give him satisfaction. The future of social work may very well be in just this area, to help people to find a new meaning in their lives through creativity, rather than provide assistance after breakdown has occurred. Those of us who work with these methods and with these measurements are confident that there is great hope for man, but this can only come about if we

begin to take a completely new and critical look at those structures and systems that society has created and which are now greatly outmoded.*

Now to come back to the angry person and the utilisation of his aggression. I met Ken in a special wing of a mental hospital designed for somewhat anti-social patients. His problem was that he could not contain his aggression, despite every attempt that had been made therapeutically. He was in his late adolescence, and his only interest was wrestling; the more violent this was, the more satisfaction he got out of it. The nurses and doctors had some anxiety about Ken and, while they did not want to give him heavy sedation, he was a constant concern because of the possibility that he might attack other patients or staff. His attitude was generally very threatening indeed.

Having learnt about his background and the problems that had led him into the hospital, we tried to explore together some ways in which this innate anger and aggression could be expressed: not in violent behaviour, but rather in some socially accepted way. He was eventually put to some demolition work which was taking place at the hospital, and also to breaking roads and putting down new surfaces. As he had to use his muscles in this 'destructive' task (like breaking the road or destroying useless buildings) he began to find a great sense of relief and began to calm down. Doctors, nurses and patients commented on how much he had changed in a relatively short space of time. This improvement was maintained, and after discharge from hospital he was helped to get work in demolition and in road work. Years later, the follow-up confirmed that Ken had been no further problem to the hospital or to the authorities. Creative, therefore, does not mean that the task in hand will necessarily be artistic.

At the very beginning of my professional career I came across a young man who had been classified as 'a bloody nuisance'. He was only twenty-one but had to be admitted

* Eugene Heimler, *Mental Illness and Social Work* (Pelican Original 1967 and 1969).

to a mental hospital because of his sadistic fantasies, with which he threatened anyone who came across him. He talked incessantly about his need to cut people up with a knife, and went into gory details of how he would do this. As he did not improve, the psychiatrist in the hospital asked me to help him find some sheltered job where he and society would be safe. Inexperienced as I was, I knew that I would not be able to help this man by psychological interpretations or words of any sort, and the longer I knew him, the less anxious I felt about the likelihood of his ever carrying out any of his threats. He confided in me and I learnt much from being with him.

Charlie (that was his name) was more bewildered by people's reactions to his fantasies than by the fantasies themselves. I wondered whether it was possible to find him a job where he could act out some of them in reality in a socially acceptable way. I thought of getting him a job in a holiday camp as a butcher, partly because he confessed how fond he was of having a good time, and partly because I thought that being a butcher might provide an outlet for his sadistic tendencies. Eventually he got such a job, and married soon afterwards. When I met Charlie a few years later he was no longer obsessed by his disturbing fantasies. He was able to *work* a great deal out of his system.

To achieve all this took a long time, and Charlie's story illustrates how, without interpreting the origin of symptoms, it was possible to enable him to live a happier life by allowing him to *use* his destructive fantasies in a harmless but useful way. It was only possible to help him through a relationship, but this was not based on interpretation of unconscious material. An analyst might have put him on the couch (had he been able to pay for the treatment over a period of years), and might thus have helped him to free himself from these destructive fantasies by tracing the symptoms to their sources in past experience. Whether or not this would have achieved more in the long run it is difficult to say. Had his symptoms been removed he would probably not have become a good butcher, but perhaps he would have done something just as satisfying.*

## 2   General Practice in Education

Those two extreme, oversimplified examples may give you the idea of how to use the 'frustration' or 'negative' to make it become 'satisfaction' or 'positive'. It may also explain what should, and eventually must, be a teacher's main function. The traditional function of teaching must give way to the teacher *facilitating* the emergence of the pupil's potential. This will mean that all education must have some *personal relevance* to the child. In consequence *the teacher must start with the child, and not with 'educating' the child.*

Traditional education assumed that there were sets of facts which children (i.e. *all* children) must know, and that these *facts* would one day help children (i.e. *all* children) to become educated adults. Of course there will be *some* children who will need facts; but all need to learn and practise responsibility; how to deal with irresponsible behaviour; how to find out what we are good at, and about the potential of our negative; how to use and share power: all this *followed* by literature, history or whatever to supply further knowledge to satisfy personal interest.

I imagine that the first year of schooling should be exploratory, allowing the teacher to get to know the child, and then, only then, to *plan education for him or her.* Basic to this education will be the recognition by the teacher that the *negative* that the child offers may one day become his or her greatest asset to society. *All education should cater for the transformation of destructive into constructive* (negative into positive) and the teacher will have to become a general practitioner in education.

The imaginative exploration of children's abilities involves the understanding that the teacher's main function is to *explore* and then to put together a syllabus to fit the child (or group of children). This, more than anything else, will lead the child in

* Heimler, *op cit.*

adult life to his or her life task – which may not be work, and may or may not find an outlet in the commercial world. Let me give an example of such exploration with a 15 year-old girl, whose overall education in the traditional sense had been satisfactory (she passed exams with good results), but who had not been prepared in any way at all to think about her own ability, her future, of what *she herself* was able to do.

The following comes verbatim from the tape. Brigitte is the facilitator in my approach. She has interviewed a number of adolescents, including Mary, who came to clarify where she might go after leaving school.

BRIGITTE:    You say you like school and you like what the future offers you. Do you know what you would like to do when you finish school?

MARY:        Yeah, I am going to university. I mean I never thought of not going to university. I think it's being expected of me.

BRIGITTE:    You think it is expected of you?

MARY:        Well, I don't know, since the age of, say, nine I have never thought of not going to university, because everybody in my family has. But I think I would like to, because it's a whole new life and I would have a lot of people of my age around to do things with. I would also love the social activity. And my sisters go to university. It seems a good idea.

BRIGITTE:    And do you know, when you go to university, what you would like to do there?

MARY:        I have no idea. Well, there is one thing I definitely won't do.

BRIGITTE:    And what is that?

MARY:        I don't want to do physics. I have given that up. That is quite surprising because both of my sisters are doing that. I am really more interested in psychology. Really, I would like to do that, perhaps.

BRIGITTE: What do you like about it. Do you know?

MARY: It will interest me because of my Mum, because my mother is a probation officer. She sort of analyses people. I find that I do that as well, and I think I can see through them quite easily. Because I was brought up with it.

BRIGITTE: So, Mary, you say that you would like to become a psychologist. How old are you now?

MARY: Fifteen.

BRIGITTE: If you put yourself ten years ahead, which is quite a long time, when you will be 25 years old, can you yourself see what you are doing, or what you would like to be doing, in the light of what you just said about psychology?

MARY: No idea. Absolutely no idea. I don't know. Perhaps that's a surprise, but I have no idea whatsoever. But I want to do something. I don't want to get married immediately, but I don't know. Not at all. No idea.

BRIGITTE: So when you say that you are interested in people and you can look through your friends quite easily. . .

MARY: I feel I would like to work like that, but I am not clever enough. I think very lowly of myself. And my parents seem to think highly of me, I don't know why, they think I am really clever, but I don't think I am.

BRIGITTE: You say you are interested in people but you are not clever enough really to do something with them?

| | |
|---|---|
| MARY: | No, I'm not. |
| BRIGITTE: | What do you feel you have not got? What would you need in order to do what you talked to me about? |
| MARY: | I don't know. I mean. . . (*long silence*) I don't know. I don't feel I'll be good enough. . . |
| BRIGITTE: | Good enough for what? |
| MARY: | I always feel I am not clever enough. There are lots of people who are cleverer, whom other people could rely on better, I should think give better advice. I don't know. |
| BRIGITTE: | You mean you are not good enough for giving advice, or they cannot rely on you? |
| MARY: | Yeah, they can rely on me! They can rely on me! I always think there would be people better than me. It would be worthwhile for them, not for me. I can't explain myself. I mean I would like to do psychology but I would feel bad. Maybe I would say the wrong things and make people worse. |
| BRIGITTE: | Well, what you are saying is that you feel you are quite good at it *now*, with your friends. |
| MARY: | Yes, I do. |
| BRIGITTE: | What would be the difference between now and ten years later? |
| MARY: | I don't know. I feel, I feel that later . . . I can't imagine myself as getting. . . I mean, each year you go to school you get cleverer each year. I think I am just as clever as I was when I was seven. I don't know how clever I get. I mean I obviously realise I am not cleverer, but I mean I obviously am, but I don't realise. . . I can't imagine |

myself as being very clever by the time I am 55 or something like that. I don't know.

BRIGITTE: If you were totally free to do something, if you were totally free to choose, what would you choose? Never mind whether you think that you can do it now or not.

MARY: If I was totally free, right? Well, I fancy working with people, I said before. But also, *I like tension. I would like to be an actress.* I don't even bother now to go through this sort of thing because there is no point really, 'cos there is so much competition.

BRIGITTE: What would you like about being an actress? If you imagine yourself in say 20 years' time, what do you see yourself doing?

MARY: I would like to act in theatre plays.

BRIGITTE: Would it matter to you what kind of role you played?

MARY: No. I like sort of playing heraldic parts. I would quite like a major role.

BRIGITTE: So you could imagine yourself being an actress and playing a major role.

MARY: Yeah.

BRIGITTE: Do you act now?

MARY: Yes, I used to be in a lot of plays at school. I like it; I enjoy it.

BRIGITTE: Mary, can you express what. . .
(*Mary suddenly gets very excited and interrupts Brigitte. Her voice changes completely.*)

MARY: *I love people watching me. I love it,* because you know everyone is concentrating on what I am doing. I suppose it's showing off. I don't know. I would enjoy it. I suppose it's because you are not yourself any more. You could be something else, like if I am a

heroine – I would love to be that!
(*Her face lights up with a big smile.*)

BRIGITTE: So you know what you would like to do?

MARY: Mmmm; but I know I won't do it.

BRIGITTE: Mary, when you gave me the answer to the question 'Does life give you enough scope for self-expression?', you said out of 20 points you would score only 8 points.

MARY: You see, to you I can express myself, but to the majority of people I can't. People don't want to know how I really feel about life. People can't be bothered with that.

BRIGITTE: Where do you feel you would like to express yourself more?

MARY: When I am with people. But when I see people putting on acts it annoys me because there is no reason why people should not be themselves, but they aren't. I am not myself when I am with people, I am sure of it. That's what I mean: *people should be themselves, but there is no room for that.*

BRIGITTE: What is it, then, that *you* would like to express more?

MARY: *To tell people how annoyed they make me.*

BRIGITTE: So you would like to tell people how you feel about them?

MARY: Yes, and how I feel if they ignore me.

BRIGITTE: Do I understand that you would like to tell people who you really are?

MARY: Yes! If I am on a one to one basis with anyone I like, then I can. I become me then, myself, whereas if I am in a crowd, it's no good. Then I take it the wrong way. (*Now Mary is blowing her nose heavily.*)

BRIGITTE: Mary, do your friends at school ever talk about what they would like to do after school?

| | |
|---|---|
| MARY: | Well, they only know that they will go to university or not. We usually talk about what is happening in our lives now, not what is going to happen. I think about the future up to the summer, or four or five months' time, but not as far as ten or twenty years. |
| BRIGITTE: | But you are having a fantasy. You say that if you were totally free to do what you would like to do, you would be an actress. |
| MARY: | Yes, I think so. Then I could express a lot that I cannot otherwise. |
| BRIGITTE: | I think you know what your dreams are, and I hope you will have the chance to really fulfill them. |
| MARY: | (*Uneasy laughter and hesitation*) I don't know! |
| BRIGITTE: | Why not? |
| MARY: | I will never be an actress! |
| BRIGITTE: | Why not? |
| MARY: | Because, because there would be lots of people who would question me. |
| BRIGITTE: | You say that you have acted before. |
| MARY: | Oh yes, I enjoy it! |
| BRIGITTE: | And have people been so much better than you? |
| MARY: | No! But that's only small numbers, that's not the majority is it? I don't know! (*With a giving-up voice*) I always imagine myself ending up behind the counter in a sweet shop. I hope this will never happen. |
| BRIGITTE: | Why wouldn't you like that? |
| MARY: | Because it is so monotonous. There is nothing to achieve there, is there really? |
| BRIGITTE: | Are you saying that you need excitement and a sense of achievement, and that you want to show yourself? |

MARY: Exactly, otherwise it would be like in a factory – I could stick to it for a while, but not for long; whereas with acting there is so much you can do. There is such a variety of things you can never get bored of it, never, never. You get different audiences and different reactions and you can make an impact on something. I quite like that.

A young student entering, say, psychology may not be sure whether her chosen field is the right one. This, by the way, also applies to many students who leave secondary school. Often the choice is haphazard, as in the case of Mary, and lack of experience, confusion about one's abilities, or the inability to relate inner problems to the outer world, may mean that the young man or woman chooses a profession which is inappropriate for him or her. The first aim of higher education should, as in the case of small children, be an exploration of how the inner self can relate to the outer. Since up to now the initial exploration for small children has not been introduced, there should be at least a year in which expressed intentions are taken both by the students and by the teachers with a 'pinch of salt'. Again, instead of bombarding the young college or university student with a set syllabus, there should be an intensive and imaginative exploration of his or her gifts, abilities, aspirations and future intentions, very much on the lines of Brigitte's interview with Mary. The tutorial system might be helpful here and, in my own experience, often is, achieving a great deal of clarification.

There are many ways and techniques by which this can be done, but the young person needs to have access to an experienced teacher or, as I said, a 'general practitioner in education', who in the first instance would see such candidates in small groups. Whether the teacher's basic education and training is in art, literature or science is less relevant than the postgraduate studies during which, whatever the basic training may be, he/she can learn about the specific approach of unearthing the 'bad' to become 'good'.

The group should be small, between 7 to 11 students; initially the topic of discussion must relate to a number of questions that the student may put,

1    In relation to the tentatively chosen field.
2    Whether or not their past experience and interest enable them to fit into that field.

One member of the group, Mary maybe, formulates a question: 'what is psychology?' or 'what does a psychologist do?' The other members of the group then respond with their understanding of psychology. There is an initial understanding that a question which has been posed by one of the group members does not need an authoritative answer, but rather that each student should express his or her understanding of what the question means to herself or himself. Answers, therefore, are not 'advice' to the questioner, but rather an expression of one's own understanding of the question.

The task of the group will be seen to be manifold. The task of the educator or facilitator will be seen to be manifold.

1    He will state the nature of the 'contract' under which the tutorial group is to operate: questions will have to be formulated by individual members, and the answers to such questions are, in fact, monologues by individuals as to their own understanding of what that question means to them.

2    The educator/facilitator will act as a synthesiser. From time to time he will sum up the essence of what has been said so far and return to the questioner for his reactions to what he has heard. He will also ask the questioner as to his feelings, whether he feels comfortable or otherwise with what has been said so far.

3 The group tutor can supply factual information as to the questions raised ('what is psychology?') and may suggest some preliminary reading on this subject. The educator will see to it that before a further question is asked, which often arises from a discussion, the questioner is fully satisfied with the reactions received.

4 Further questions can then be formulated and answered in a somewhat similar fashion.

Apart from written material, imaginative video tape presentations would be adaptable to group tutorials. It is important that such visual presentations should not be further discussions of lectures, but should be action-orientated. For example, groups of students may wish to view experienced psychologists in action in various settings of psychology. Afterwards further tutorials could, and no doubt would, deal with some of the reactions and questions which arise from the observation of this video tape material. Such material could also include interviews with psychologists about their satisfactions and frustrations, problems and solutions in relation to their professional work. It should also be available to cover a wide field of settings, i.e. factories, offices, mines, oil plants, etc. For example, if the students have been observing the psychologist interviewing a postman, some videotape material could be available for the life, working and private, of postmen. If, during the videotape presentation, the postman should refer to, say inadequate working conditions, subsequent tutorials might deal with the trades union aspect of the postman's dilemma, bringing into the tutorial knowledgeable people on this subject.

In short, a basic question such as 'what is psychology?' may lead far and wide; and the various components, as one pattern leads to another, will make the whole issue of learning a creative and interesting one. Learning then evolves through the interest of individual students. There will be students who will be less interested in, say, the trades union's aspects of the postman's dilemma than in his hobbies and interests. Further videotape material should then be available to deal with the wide field of leisure activities, and teachers and others who would be able to discuss these aspects with the students could be brought into the group. If Mary, for example, were led to recognise that her ability may not lie in direct work with people or acting but, say, in literature, art or, for that matter, engineering, then she should have access to group advisers who would similarly explore her questions in these alternative fields and supply answers in a similar manner as described before.

Perhaps I ought to point out that *interest* in a particular subject or work does not necessarily correspond with *ability*. In order to get to the ability the teacher/facilitator must deal with the underlying negatives.*

Eighteen years ago my colleague, the late Louise Dighton, and I, while being involved with the Hounslow Project, interviewed a great many children in various schools. We found then, as Brigitte finds now, a great lack of understanding of children's needs, particularly in helping them to formulate feasible plans for their future. Most children have little opportunity to express their dreams, their personality traits, in connection with choosing a career or life task. Aptitude tests may express what a young person *could* be good at, without considering the emotional factors, the most important creative force in career selection. What we found in those days was that the Careers Adviser responded to questions from the child like, 'Tell me, sir, how can I become an electrician?' Or the Careers Adviser would ask the child if he would be interested in, say, work as an account-

* For further details see Eugene Heimler, *Survival in Society* (Weidenfeld & Nicolson, 1975; Eugene Heimler Foundation and Cardwell Human Resources, 1983)

ant, or as a mechanic in a garage, and so on. Academic achievements, or lack of them, defined which way the Careers Adviser
would make 'the cookie crumble', but the creative, emotional
side of the child, in the sense outlined here so far, was not
considered. Academic achievement alone does not equal
creativity, nor does the lack of such achievement indicate the
opposite. The world of work and life task towards the twenty-
first century demands, as we have seen, new skills for the
educator; and also, as I said before, a totally different syllabus.
We must at last realise the following:

1   Work, *as we know* it, will not be available for millions of
people. They will need life tasks.
2   What remains of 'work' will be shifted into certain areas like
*engineering, personal services* (leisure, holiday, etc), *human relations
trainers* (covering some of the aspects and more mentioned in
this book, including the GP in education), *life task facilitators*
(assisting in the selection and training of the unemployed and
redundant), *accountants, lawyers, nurses, transport drivers, enter-
tainers, small businesses* (involving the various members of the
family), *computer information, personal services* for the aged and the
sick (more about this later in this chapter), *relaxation services*
(keep fit, drama, painting, writing, art classes). Some (but not
all) of these headings are also stated by the US Bureau of
Labour in their prediction for the 80s. This list is by no means
complete, but it may give a clue to the ways in which the GP
Educator will need to cast his attention.
3   Employment as the main societal structure will give way to
various forms of traditional and imaginative self-employment.
Most people will not even want 'jobs' after a while!
4   People who are 'unemployed' will be given funds in order to
do things rather than to do nothing. This would replace the
present Unemployment Benefit for the able-bodied young who
would be willing to participate in a new scheme, and would
allow them to earn some extra money, too.

Alvin Toffler in his book *The Third Wave* says that the crisis of change is not new in Western society, that a similar, great upheaval hit society with the onset of the Industrial Revolution, when peasants had to leave the fields and move into crowded factories. A whole way of life was turned upside down. There are no signs today; 'Ye are entering the Post-Industrial age!', yet teachers of the young should have this sign in the classrooms of our schools to do justice to their profession and not to forget *in which age* they are teaching!

## 3   Life Task

The term 'life task' as used in these pages denotes the alternative to traditional working and employment. Alfred Adler, who coined it, understood by it a set of responsibilities in relation to work, marriage and friendship. Whether governments and trades unions admit it or not, work and employment as we know them will not apply to an increasing number of people who at present are 'on the dole' and *not allowed* to engage in paid or unpaid activities.

Thinking in terms of a 'life task' would mean that, after thorough exploration in school, the young man or woman would know what kind of training to seek out, and that this training would be well organised and available for his or her needs. It would mean that he or she would be trained over a period of time, not necessarily to enter the traditional job market, but, for instance, to offer her or his services to two large groups in the community: the aged and the sick.* In our society these groups cannot afford many of the products or services on the open competitive market, so in consequence they go without many of the basic comforts that others can take for granted. Not only have the unemployed young been thrown on to the rubbish heap of society, but the old as well. Now the young and the old (and sick) would cater for each other's needs – one supplying

* for other 'life task' suggestions, see p. 114 below.

the various services, and the other receiving them. Such services would be as manifold as the training of the young, from various repair work to ingenious innovation (like the supplying of battery-fed pads for the relief of rheumatism or arthritis, or the making of individually-designed orthopaedic shoes, etc.).

The training and services would be subsidised by government in the first instance by transferring funds at present used for Unemployment Benefit and Social Security (to the able-bodied young) to voluntary organisations, who in turn would pay wages for services rendered to the aged and sick. The latter two would also contribute a *minimum* for such services. There would hardly be any competition with the open market, as neither the old nor the sick can at present afford *any* services from them, and the trades unions, I believe, once they registered the facts of a changed age, would not consider this solution in the same way as they do some of the present government schemes with their 'cheap labour' aspects. This new scheme would benefit their own retired and sick members, as well as providing the human concern for working people, which has always been the ideal of the trades union movement in Britain. The *basis* for such new endeavours could be new types of cottage industries for repairs, operating from the homes of the individuals, who would get their work referred from *local* central bases of such 'cottages'.

On more conventional lines, there are the service industries – the bus, train, postal and other services so very necessary to the running of a modern society – which are at present being run down and becoming highly inefficient, with fewer and fewer staff. There is plenty of scope for the government to encourage more people to make a determined and creative contribution to them.

Again, people with training could be encouraged to go out and help in the developing countries, in an extension of the present Voluntary Service Overseas organisation.

## 4  Alternative Life Tasks

Service and caring skills, however, may not be everyone's pre-
ference. Many may find that the coming new age will allow and
encourage activities which are at present outside the possibilities of many men and women. On p.111 I mentioned *Relaxation
Services*, and the various classes where learning takes place in art
subjects. But what happens when the learning is over? So far,
entertainment, for example, has taken place in somewhat traditional settings in theatres. There is already a new developing
form of entertainment in many big cities where young people
produce spontaneous entertainment of various kinds (Covent
Garden is one such place). To date, however, these still smack
of charity, due to the fact that the onlookers are invited to place
money in a hat or plate. If, however, designated places were
made available by the different municipal authorities for the
purposes of short public entertainments, many young people
would be able to perform, and would also receive some re-
muneration from tickets sold. But in any case, is it not better for
the individual and society if people perform, rather than sit and
brood at home, or, in a state of despair, commit anti-social acts?
Local Authorities need to provide some structure, some organisation, so that these activities may be engaged in on a more
regular basis. Nothing is more morale-boosting than to be able
to use one's abilities and be appreciated for them.

In Seattle, Washington, USA, in 1979, I was invited to talk
with a group of drug addicts. Without exception they had been
heavy drug users, and had great difficulties in breaking away
from this body- and soul-destroying habit. As it happened, a
number of treatment centres for drug addiction in Seattle were
the responsibility of a former actress who had also had training
in my approach. She made contact with the Professor of Drama
at the local university, and they joined forces to teach many of
these drug addicts first to *act* and then to *perform* to ordinary
audiences at the University Theatre. The results, according to
what these addicts told me, were little short of amazing. They
claimed that the two interacting processes of learning the disci-

pline of acting and placing themselves under the skin of the character, and *then* appearing in public, had a greater effect on their recovery than anything else they received in the way of treatment.

If acting, for example, has such a dramatic impact on people who have been ill for a very long time, would it have less effect on the healthy whose life task might be to perform? Many of our schools, colleges and universities have their own theatres, often under-used. With some financial help and organisation, a new creative possibility could be realised.

Other areas which might be explored include those of the creative arts, again partly on the analogy of my experience of therapeutic treatments. Many years ago, when I was at the beginning of my professional career, I came across an ingenious DRO (Disablement Rehabilitation Officer), who encouraged some of the disabled to produce various items, from toys to artistic work, and organised exhibitions and sales. At that time this was not yet done by many of his other colleagues, although I understand that later some other DROs followed suit. If the unemployed were offered the financial support to organise themselves similarly, their work could reach large sections of the public and could be sold. Already there are very successful street and covered markets all over the United Kingdom, where young people who have managed to find some financial backing, or who started up while still working in another job, sell their artefacts to passersby. It is a matter of getting started. In one of the London Boroughs I recently met a group of young men and women who had considerable musical gifts and wanted to produce their own records. They needed only a relatively small sum to enable them to do so, but alas, it was not available! With subsidies for the unemployed to engage in silversmithing, carpentry, leatherwork, ceramics, jewellery, painting, sculpture, wood-carving, photography and such, we might perhaps even precipitate a new renaissance of the arts.

The long and short of what I am saying is that *not only is there a need for the economic distribution of human energy to enable us to live a full*

*life, but there has to be a new economic distribution of financial resources
to enable people to use their potentials.*

## 5 Politicians' Comments and the Future

On 4 October 1984 the latest unemployment figures showed
that 13.6 per cent of the working population was unemployed.
A number of politicians of various parties were interviewed, and
without exception they said that in time we should return to
improved or even full employment. Some said that the present
grave situation was partly due to the increase in the population,
and to the fact that we were becoming less competitive. They
were very concerned about the rising unemployment because it
was felt that we could not sustain a prolonged period of it and
hope to keep society stable. Some called for large-scale spend-
ing on capital projects like road works, sewer replacement and
expansion of the railways. No reference was made to the fact
that the present crisis is not limited to Britain, that we are facing
a worldwide phenomenon, that we have, without fanfares,
entered the post-industrial age.

Of course, it is difficult for politicians to state publicly that
*there are no real answers*, as there were in the past, and to accept
that from now on we need to deal with work and worklessness in
a completely new way. We have been so conditioned to 'work'
in the traditional sense that our politicians do not even dare to
think and state any alternative. Meanwhile the older unemployed feel a sense of shame and uselessness, but not the
young. They speak about the heart- and body-breaking slavery
of nine to five, every day, for fifty years. They claim something
more, much more, for themselves and see in the emerging new
technology a chance for a new kind of life. Our politicians, with
the best of intentions, do not look towards the future; they are
stuck in the past, while the future slowly unfolds with a great
deal of upheaval and pain. Sooner or later the realisation will
come, of course; but in the meantime, with the fragmented
schemes that are available, they are only dealing with the
visible part of the unemployment iceberg.

There needs to be, as I said before, an economic distribution of financial resources to:

1   explore in imaginative ways and in schools the hidden potential of our young.
2   when the potential is clearly identified, then, *irrespective of the need of the market economy*, to give training to young women and men to realise their potentials. Unlike the present *one-year* youth training scheme (which causes a great deal of anxiety due to the uncertainty of whether or not a job waits at the end of the tunnel) *every* young man or woman would have a clearly defined function, either in the market economy or in what I termed life tasks.

If the choice is to be the life task activity, either directed towards the elderly and sick or in some other expression of creative activity, provisions will have to be made for a structured and planned base or organisation to make possible the delivery of services or creative activities.

3   Funds must be made available by government through voluntary organisations replacing Unemployment Benefit for the able-bodied, augmented by the contribution given by the users.
4   This plan needs the closest co-operation between government, voluntary organisations and trades unions.

What makes the deepening crisis worse is that parties are trying to make political capital out of it. Unemployment and redundancy, they say, will be over in time, and they paint a picture of the return to the 'fleshpots of Egypt'. This false promise complicates matters a great deal, because it forces millions of people, including the young, to feel useless, anxious, bitter and depressed.

One day, when we have reached the promised land of creative living, we shall look back into the second part of the twentieth century and wonder why it took so long, with so much pain and misery, to recognise the freedom and the potential that unemployment, redundancy and stagnation may offer to millions. We shall recognise that the 'good life' is to fulfil to the greatest extent possible the gifts which have lain dormant in us since the Industrial Revolution.

# 7 Information and Training in the Heimler Method

*A Short History of the Method**

While working with unemployed men and women in the 1950s, I needed some structured way to understand the gravity of the problems of the unemployed. This structure, consisting of a number of experiments in 'community care', i.e. the care of people outside hospitals, carried out by local authority mental health departments, was undertaken by Middlesex County Council between 1953 and 1965. The first of such experiments was in conjunction with the National Assistance Board and concerned the long term unemployed.†

As a result of this experiment, the National Assistance Board initiated training courses in Human Relations at the Department of Extra-mural Studies at the University of London in 1958. A one-and-a-half hour session per week was held throughout the academic year.‡ All these courses were for Executive and Higher Executive officers of the Board.

Soon ten other universities elsewhere in the country joined in, and the Annual Report of the National Assistance Board in 1964 stated that 1,300 Executive and Higher Executive officers had taken that course. By 1962 similar courses were in operation for personnel of the Ministry of Labour, and about 70 Ministry of Labour officials had joined our ranks.

Further development arose from the original Hendon Experiment with long-term unemployed. In 1963–4 the instructors

* The name of the method used to be Human Social Functioning. It is now increasingly known as the Heimler Method.
† See Eugene Heimler, 'Psychiatric Social Work with National Assistance Board Cases' in *The Medical Officer,* 16 December 1965 (94, pp 351-353)
‡ Eugene Heimler, 'Looking Behind the Cold Facts' in *New Society*, 18 April 1963

of the National Assistance Board (instructing new entrants to the Board and carrying out refresher courses for Executive officers, etc.) took a year's training under my guidance, so that in consequence they could pass this on to new entrants and others in their teaching work. A syllabus emerged which became an integral part of the curriculum of the training of the National Assistance Board in Hinchley Wood. (This was at that time a government training centre.) Finally, specialised Welfare Officers of the Board have been taking courses to enable them to deal with particularly difficult unemployment problems with greater awareness and in more concentrated fashion. Orientation courses were also held for Regional Controllers and Managers of the Board throughout the country.

Investigating the emotional significance that work had for people*, I began to realise as the year went by that in order to understand the full significance of work, or for that matter the ability or inability to function in society, I had to try to find out the relationship between those people who returned to useful long-term work and those who did not. Thus, by 1961 I had evaluated 1,200 recipients of the Board to see whether or not they were functioning in society.† I came to realise that those who did function received more satisfaction out of life than those who did not. By 1962 I was fairly certain that there were five areas of human needs or satisfactions which had to be translated into sub-sections before they could be scored on a point system. (See Chapter 3.)

After the Hendon Experiment I moved to the London Borough of Hounslow to carry out, among other things, research which was given the name 'the Hounslow Project'. It was here in this London Borough that validations on my Scale started in this country and encouraged others to use it in other parts of the world. By 1968 a number of professionals were using

---

* Eugene Heimler, 'The Emotional Significance of Work' in *The Medical Officer*, 16 August 1957 (98, pp 96-98)
†The term 'functioning' refers to a satisfaction/frustration ratio in overall favour of satisfactions.

my Scale and reports came in that the use of the Scale could save several hours interviewing time (apart from the involvement of the clients in their own recovery).*

Developments abroad were very considerable. Centres for studies in Social Functioning were established in the states of Washington and California and work was carried out with the unemployed population, with family problems, and problems of delinquency and race relations, and gradually students began to learn about the Scale and its associated methods and techniques at various North American universities. The Department of Immigration and Manpower in Western Canada began to teach their staff the concept and practice of Social Functioning.

At present the method is taught and practised in Britain (where there is a British Association of Social Functioning), in West Germany, Belgium, Holland, at several centres in Canada, including French speaking Montreal, and the United States, Japan, South Africa and New Zealand; also in Bermuda, where most of the Ministry of Social Welfare professional staff have received training.

*How does the method work?*

As I said earlier, the approach and the Scale grew primarily out of work with the unemployed. It is not so much psychotherapy but rather a new form of educational methodology to help people to learn about themselves and then use their experiences in a fairly structured and concise way. From the beginning of its development it was *reality-orientated* with limited sessions of between 6 to 12.

When I see people, they have usually contacted me by letter prior to coming. They will state what their problems are and describe briefly whether or not they have had treatment in the past. The first three sessions are exploratory. During this time we establish together what we will be aiming at in connection with the problem which is often identified by me as a potential.

* 'The Health Services of Hounslow', 1968, Department of Health publication.

Once this is established I usually offer the sessions, aiming at the resolution of the problem by turning the handicap into an asset. I find that the most important part of my work with these men and women is during the *action* itself i.e. when they are *doing* something definite and realistic. During the process of exploration I usually use my Scale so that the individual concerned can see his or her life as a whole, rather than be hypnotised by the temporary problem or crisis that she/he is experiencing. During this exploration my aim is to 'feed back' as much information as possible about the positive and negative content that is presented, and I refrain from giving an opinion or interfering in any way with the individual's free flow of communication. Without this human accepting and understanding attitude it would be impossible for him or her to open up. During this time, in order to make connections between past and present, I may use some of the techniques that I described in this book, and also some more.

In the second part I become much more active. This is during the period of *action*, when the individual is choosing his or her way of resolving these issues in reality. I may explore with him/her alternative possibilities, or even make suggestions. These, however, are clearly understood by both of us to be such, and are not advice but rather a testing procedure. During this time I often hear: 'I don't know if I can or want to do what you said, but . . .' and then come alternative suggestions, often even decisions. These must then be tested out and acted upon. My function comes to a natural end when the proposed action is carried out, with the result that not only the present situation of the individual is resolved, but he or she is able to use the creative child in him or her. Once we get to this point my work is clearly over.

Sometimes it is very useful to bring together into a group a number of men and women who have some common problems and gifts. We organise intensive sessions over two or three days, to try to deal effectively during that time with the issues presented. During this time the group and I will spend something like 10 to 15 hours together, and for many members of the group this can be just as effective as individual sessions carried over 10 to 12 weeks. Although the pace is quicker than in the individual sessions, the fact that the other members of the group are presenting their problems can be a source, a confirmation for one's emerging decisions and give considerable encouragement. In two or three days a great deal can be achieved but as the action apart will be outside the group sessions, some participants may return for individual sessions afterwards.

The size of the group depends on the nature of the problem, taking into special consideration whether the participants feel at home more in smaller or larger groups.

*Training*

The Heimler Foundation offers training for those qualified and working in one of the 'helping professions'. The basic training consists of 60 hours plus supervision, and takes place every year in August in London. This training will give the practitioners a basic knowledge in the method. In addition, personal interviews help to clarify the students' own frustrations and satisfactions and help to transform these into creativity.

The Scale is copyright and is only available to those who have undergone recognised tuition by a recognised training centre.

After the basic training and supervision, the equivalent of 12 weeks of advanced training could follow to enable the practitioner to achieve more advanced competence. Some professional men and women (including teachers) may follow courses leading to a lectureship. These are available every year during the month of August. Details about consultation and training in Britain and abroad can be obtained from the Heimler Foundation, The Manor House, 80 East End Road, London N3 2SY.

*Epilogue*

## The Meaning of the Whole

We need a certain amount of satisfaction for our survival, to fulfil certain basic needs, but it also appears that we need some frustration as well, a spur for further creative activity. If this frustration is overwhelming, then we need help to transform it into satisfaction, and if it is too little, help may equally be needed, because then nothing inspires us. This help I described as self-help because it is my professional and personal experience that, given 'the tools', many people can sort out considerable problems themselves. One of the ways in which we can attempt to do this is to understand ourselves, but self-understanding and the understanding of others run parallel.

All the case histories written down in this book came from people to whom I or my colleagues have talked. We used with them the methods described here and asked them the same questions that I have included in this book. I hope that by now some of you have answered some of your own questions, carried out some of my suggestions, and have been able to isolate and crystallise your difficulties and possibilities in connection with unemployment, redundancy and stagnation. Face to face with your problem in all its starkness, I hope you can think of possible action to take. Once you have acted you will be less frustrated or bewildered and no longer emotionally upset. Instead you are on the road to becoming an independent person in charge of your life, despite all the upheavals of your work situation.

So far I have stressed the importance of action in freeing yourself from disturbing emotions. I came to the conclusion that many of our difficulties stem from the fact that we are unable to make decisions. Therefore action can be, and often is, the end of feeling persecuted by your work situation or un-employment. With self understanding, decision, and action in sight you can free yourself from the confusion and fog that often make us lose our way in life, particularly when our livelihood is at stake. If you can eventually *use* your feelings towards a realistic solution of your predicament in connection with your work (or workless) situation, then you may find the gift that unemployment can offer you, and of which you may not have been aware.

# Index